Return to
April 1987

CHRIST IN YOUR LIFE

What God's Good News Can Do for You

Leslie Brandt

Illustrated by James Cummins

Other books by Leslie F. Brandt

PROPHETS/NOW
JESUS/NOW
EPISTLES/NOW
PSALMS/NOW
WHY DID THIS HAPPEN TO ME?
GOD IS HERE—LET'S CELEBRATE!
GOOD LORD, WHERE ARE YOU?
GREAT GOD, HERE I AM
LIVING THROUGH LOVING
PRAISE THE LORD!

Concordia Publishing House, St. Louis, Missouri
Copyright © 1980 Concordia Publishing House
Manufactured in the United States of America

Library of Congress Cataloging in Publication Data

Brandt, Leslie F.
    Christ in my life.

    1. Bible. N.T. Gospels—Meditations.
2. Christian life—1960— I. Title.
BS2555.4.B7   248'.4   79-19963
ISBN 0-570-03292-X

Foreword

It is always reassuring to know that someone else has coped with the questions we face and has found answers to them. It is good to find a path that someone else has blazed through a dense forest.

This is one of the gifts author Leslie Brandt offers the reader of this book. He tells what God's Good News has done for him as a typical human being confronted by the same kinds of problems. He knows what happens to a person when Christ enters and takes control of his or her life.

These contemplations encourage others to allow God's Word as revealed through the Scriptures to convince, console, and challenge them. It is demonstrably true, the author maintains, that when Christ lives in us, all things become new, life's perspective is changed, and life, the world, and history take on a meaning they never had for us before.

What happened to the author, and to the many others in history like him, can also happen to you: a miracle, a transformation, a redirection, and a life sustained by a sturdy, living hope. It has to, for it comes from the Creator Himself addressed to you.

The Publisher

Contents

The Consequences of Christmas

Matthew 2:1-12

Historian Charles Beard was once asked,
  "How long would it take you to tell
  all you have learned
  from your lifetime's study of history?"
He summed it up in four sentences:
  Whom the gods would destroy,
    they first make mad with power.
  The mills of God grind slowly,
    but they grind exceedingly small.
  The bee fertilizes the flower it robs.
  When it is dark enough, you see the stars.
  "When it is dark enough, you see the stars."

Robert Browning, in a burst of optimism, once wrote,
  "God is in His heaven; all's right with the world."
An American soldier during WWII responded by saying,
  "God is in His heaven alright,
    but all's riot with the world."
Sindbad the Sailor once anchored his boat
  on what appeared to be an island
  only to find that it was a great beast of the sea
  that went charging off with him, boat, and all
  across the raging ocean.
"Everything nailed down is comin' loose,"
  said the Angel Gabriel in the dramatic production
    Green Pastures.
International relations, economic conditions,
  and moral customs are inconstant and confused.
Like a great beast plunging through the sea,
  the things I have clung to and trusted in
    are sweeping me with them
  into the tumult and tempest
    of a universal storm
  that has left me grabbing frantically

at straws in the wind.
I think it surely is dark enough; where are the stars?

A star did break out of the night some 2,000 years ago.
It was *the* Star.
Prophesied by Isaiah centuries before it appeared,
    it was to bring light and hope into the Jewish world
    and, as the apostle Paul later proclaimed,
    it was meant for the Gentiles as well.
Three foreign wise men or kings observed that Star.
They remembered the ancient prophecy
    and determined to follow its rays
        and discover its meaning.

Some exciting things happened
    to these sojourners of the night.
They met Christ.
"And going into the house they saw the child with Mary,
    His mother, and they fell down and worshiped Him."
It was a summit meeting of the highest caliber—
    three kings on their knees before the King of kings.
I wonder: Has the night been dark enough
    for me to see the Star?
Or have I been so occupied with other things,
    such as the foolish tinsel of this life,
        that I am blind and numb to the darkness and loneliness
        of a life apart from Christ?
Has something taken the place of God and His purposes
    in my life?
Is someone or something else on the throne of my heart?

They gave Him gifts.
"Then, opening their treasures, they offered Him gifts,
    gold and frankincense and myrrh."
I am fully aware of the high cost of living.
I am not so nearly aware of the high cost of loving.
"God so loved the world that He gave His only Son. . . ."
This is the ultimate example of love,

and it is the pattern and model of the kind of love
that I am enjoined to manifest
in response to God's love for me.
This love begins with God.
It continues in the lives of men and women
who have accepted God's love through Christ
and who thereby become
channels and vehicles of love
to the human family about them.
Once I realize God's great, eternal love,
I will become a lover,
and my love for God—and my gifts to God—
are to be offered to Him by way of the altar
of my neighbor's need.
God does not want only what is mine; He wants me.
My response to God's love is the giving of myself
to Him and to others on His behalf.
This is the meaning of worship—
the offering of myself to God.

They walked a new path.
"And being warned in a dream not to return to Herod,
they departed to their own country by another way."
This symbolizes what happens—or ought to happen—
to every person who meets Christ.
"If anyone is in Christ," wrote the apostle Paul,
"he is a new creation; the old has passed away,
behold the new has come."
If I plunge into the new year determined
to walk in old paths,
paths of selfishness, deceit, fear, anxiety, despair,
it indicates that Christmas has done little for me,
that I have not really met and worshiped
the Christ of Christmas or, having met Him,
am not consistently following Him.

A new life means a new walk.
The most radical thing that can happen to a person,
whether he or she is fully conscious of it or not,
happens when that person becomes a Christian,

when the Christ born in Bethlehem
is born in his or her heart.
New goals, new attitudes, new motivations
gradually begin to take over
and take the place of those selfish ambitions
that once mastered his or her life.
This is what happens when those
amidst this world's darkness
see that bright Star of the East,
bask in its warmness, thrill to its cheer,
and kneel in loving adoration before its Christ.
God grant that I meet and receive Him in worship,
give myself to Him in loving surrender,
and walk in the paths that He sets before me.

Consecrating the Commonplace

John 2:1-11

I live with three- and four-inch headlines.
People about me think in superlatives.
They act in terms of that which is the best,
    the greatest, the most glamorous,
        fantastic, incredible.
Even the church, unless it produces entertainment
    comparable to a Hollywood premier
    or the excitement of healing and holy-rolling,
    will seldom get a rise out of the average citizen
    on main street or in the marketplace.

It is paradoxically significant
    that Jesus' first recorded manifestation
    of divine power and glory
    was among the commonplace circumstances
        of a dinner party.
Whereas Christ's other miracles, for the most part,
    dealt with particularly difficult and painful problems,
    His very first work of wonder is performed
    in a very ordinary and joyful situation
    which hardly required the service of a supernatural God.
A less reverent reader of the Bible
        might crassly suppose
    that Jesus was timidly trying out His magic
        on a small scale
    before taking on more fantastic acts
    like healing lepers and giving sight to the blind
        and raising the dead.
The fact remains, however, that this Jesus
    who refused to turn stones into bread
        to satiate His own hunger
    did not hesitate to convert water into wine
        to further the enjoyment
    of a crowd of merrymakers and wedding guests.

The first encouraging revelation of this incident
    in the ministry of Jesus
  is the promise that *the glory and splendor,*
    the power and might of God,
  are available and applicable
  within the ordinary, commonplace, routine
  circumstances of everyday living.
The first followers of Christ discovered this
  through actual experience in their lives.
"So, whether you eat or drink, or whatever you do,
    do all to the glory of God,"
  wrote Paul to the Christians at Corinth.
"I can do all things in Him who strengthens me,"
  he said in another of his letters.
He found that Christ and His divine power was as available
  to him in prison as it was when he was among
  his Christian friends.
It is no wonder that he could state with confidence:
    "My God will supply every need of yours
    according to His riches in glory in Christ Jesus."
How rich my life would become if I could grasp
  the significance of this splendid truth!
The Psalmist, in one of his more optimistic moments,
  realized this.
"Thou dost beset me behind and before,
  and layest Thy hand upon me," he said.
"If I ascend to heaven, Thou art there!
If I make my bed in Sheol, Thou art there!
If I take the wings of the morning
  and dwell in the uttermost parts of the sea,
  even there Thy hand shall lead me,
  and Thy right hand shall hold me."

What ought all this mean to me?
It means that the commonplace task need no longer
  be common or mundane.
Whether it be within the realm of tedious housework,
  or the drab duty of selling merchandise,
  or running an office, working in a factory,

or teaching a group of rowdy children,
the presence of Christ blesses and clothes it
with prestige and purpose.
Jesus is able to work miracles
in my most ordinary circumstances,
thereby transforming the day's drudgery and routine
into vehicles of blessing and abundance
for me and for others about me.
This is incredibly true!
Jesus hallows every corner of human life—of my life—
with His perpetual presence.

I believe that Christ's first miracle demonstrates,
at least symbolically,
His purpose and power in transforming
earthly pleasures into eternal joy.
He is not a joy-killer
whose presence stifles my happiness
or cuts short my pleasures.
He seeks rather to ennoble and enhance these things
and make them stepping-stones
to a true and everlasting joy.
I know what happens when someone plunges a lighted candle
into a jar of oxygen.
Something like this happens when Christ is invited
into my human enjoyments and earthly pleasures.
His miracle-working power can take the water
of my temporal pleasures
and transform it into the rich wine
of perpetual and eternal joy.
"Thou dost show me the path of life," said the psalmist;
" . . . in Thy right hand are pleasures for evermore."
"Take delight in the Lord," he further exhorts,
"and He will give you the desires of your heart."
"These things I have spoken to you," said Jesus,
"that My joy may be in you and
that your joy may be full."

The legitimate pleasures about me are good.
They are the gifts of a loving heavenly Father.

They are to be used and enjoyed.
I am, however, never to be satisfied with these alone.
They are only a prelude to that life and experience
    of absolute and eternal joy
    which is found only in a right relationship
        with Jesus Christ.
Jesus has come to change or transform
    all of the less sweet, satisfying pleasure-draughts
        which I take from earth's cisterns
    into the joyous wine
        of His kingdom.

Jesus' first miracle manifests *His divine glory*
    in a beautiful demonstration
    of His willingness and readiness
    to overcome my deficiencies and lack
    with His supernatural and eternal power and provision.
"The mother of Jesus said to Him, 'They have no wine.'"
By an act of will Jesus changed plain water into rich wine,
    thereby supplying the needs of the guests.
The same power which He so aptly displayed here
    is still ready and waiting to be exercised
    on behalf of His believing children.
I need not see Him with my eyes
    or touch Him with my hands
    to know His love and care.
This Christ who, without pomp or ceremony,
    created the best wine of the feast after the natural,
    ordinary supply was consumed,
    will give to me and all His followers,
    if we will but receive,
    a fountain of living water or wine
    which will supply our needs long after our natural
    or human resources have been exhausted.
When the world's platters are empty,
    the cups drained dry,
    the Lord God promises to feed and satisfy
    the immortal hunger and the insatiable thirst
    of every spirit who longs for Him.

"This, the first of His signs, Jesus did
   at Cana of Galilee,
   and manifested His glory;
   and His disciples believed in Him."
A miracle was wrought not only with water and wine
      in that day,
   but in the hearts of those few who had begun
      to follow Him.
The water of their tiny faith was transformed
   into the wine of a nobler and more devoted faith—
   a faith which ultimately turned them
   into history-changing, world-shaking personalities
   that inaugurated the church that I am a part of today.

Now, if the disciples believed in Jesus
      as a result of this miracle,
   how dare I doubt who have been a witness
   to countless scores of miracles that have been performed
   in the name of and by the power of
   this same Christ throughout the ages?
Is it possible that I still don't fully trust
   this Great One who brings His divine power to bear
   upon all aspects of human life,
   who enters my joys and sorrows,
   who anticipates and responds to my every need,
   who stands ready to fill my every lack out of His
   inexhaustible and all-sufficient fullness?
I need, again and again, to lay claim and commit myself
   to this wonderful Christ and allow Him to transform
   the polluted and bitter waters of my life
   into the rich wine of His eternal fullness and joy.
And I need this not for myself alone,
   but for my discordant world
      and its distraught inhabitants
   whom I am called and commissioned to serve.

Divine Power for Daily Living

Matthew 8:1-13

I live in a discordant, disjointed, tragic,
    sin-ridden world.
The seed of sin and death, and the pain and suffering
    that accompanies it, is deep within me.
It shall be so until I discard my mortal body
    to become totally and perfectly united with God.
Nevertheless, I have already been delivered
    from sin's guilt and eternal consequences
    and been granted everlasting life
    through the resurrected Christ.
The joy of that deliverance does not, however,
    exempt me from pain and suffering in this life.
The fire and the crucible are often necessary
    to mature and sanctify me
    as God's servant in my kind of world.
Yet the divine, supernatural, miracle-working power of God
    is ready and available in my every circumstance—
    to enable me to bear the pain and to forge it
    into a vehicle or vessel that will serve His purposes
        in and through my life—
    or to deliver me and set me free
    from whatever may hurt or hinder His purposes
        in and through me.

The power that cured the leper of his leprosy
    and delivered the servant of the centurion
        of his paralysis
    is the same power that is available and applicable
        to me today.
And this is available and applicable whatever my needs
    or problems or sicknesses.
My responsibility is to learn how to latch on to it
    and to make it work for me—and for God—
    in my difficult circumstances.

The characters and incidents of this Gospel lesson
    give me some direction as to how I can make
    divine grace and power applicable to my circumstances.

First of all, *I must honestly and boldly acknowledge*
    my particular need or needs.
The leper recognized his need:
    "Lord, if You will, you can make me clean,"
        he exclaimed.
The centurion came to Christ
    on behalf of someone else's need:
    "Lord, my servant is lying paralyzed at home,
        in terrible distress."
The psalmist of the Old Testament acknowledged
    the problems that he could not handle in his life:
"Save me, O God, for the waters have come up to my neck.
I sink in deep mire, where there is no foothold;
    I have come into deep waters,
    and the flood sweeps over me. . . ."
God met his need:
"I waited patiently for the Lord;
    He inclined to me and heard my cry.
He drew me up from the desolate pit,
        out of the miry bog,
    and set my feet upon a rock,
        making my steps secure."
"Wretched man that I am!" wrote the apostle Paul;
    "who will deliver me from this body of death?"
He knew the answer to his own excruciating query:
    "Thanks be to God through Jesus Christ our Lord!"

Whether it be the Psalmist, Paul, or the characters
    of this Gospel lesson, they had problems or needs
    that they could not handle by themselves.
In their acknowledgement of this,
    they opened up their lives
    to the intervention of God.
It is this confrontation with myself
    and my particular problem,

this acknowledgement of my need,
  that is necessary to prepare the way
    for God's intervention in my life.

Having honestly faced up to my problem and need
  and having come to the end of myself and my sufficiency
  in dealing with my problem or need,
  I must request and embrace
  God's available power and grace.
The "leper came to Jesus and knelt before Him. . . ."
The "centurion came forward to Him, beseeching Him. . . ."
Christians are often comparable
  to a millionaire who starves to death
  because he doesn't have enough sense
  to go to a bank and cash a check.
They "do not have because they do not ask."
"Ask and you will receive," said Jesus.
God's grace and power, His help and healing,
  His divine solutions to human problems,
  are available and applicable for the complex,
  painful, crippling problems of my life.
I don't have to continue carrying on in my uncertain,
  fearful world within my poverty-stricken human resources.
The riches of heaven, the divine power of God,
  are at my disposal.
I need only to claim those riches—and enjoy them.
The submission of my need or problem to God, however,
  must be accompanied by the submission of my life
    to Him and His purposes.
I can hardly expect God to grant me power and grace
  simply to enable me to continue on in my sinful,
    self-centered ways.
I am His workmanship,
  "created in Christ Jesus for good works," wrote Paul,
  "which God prepared beforehand,
    that we should walk in them."
There must be request for and acceptance of
    God's gracious gifts—
  and obedience to His will and purpose for my life—

if His divine power is to be applied to and channeled
through my life.

Having requested and accepted God's miracle-working power
for the solving of specific problems,
the exorcising of demons, the healing of sicknesses,
and having truly submitted my life
to God's ownership and control,
I must carry on as if the request had been granted
and God-given power is at work in and through me.
The leper may not immediately have realized
the full extent of his cure,
but Christ enjoined him to act as if it had happened:
"Go, show yourself to the priest,
and offer the gift that Moses commanded,
for a proof to the people."
The man took Jesus at His word and took off—
in obedience to His command—
as if God's healing power had already been granted.
The Roman centurion expressed such superb confidence
in Christ's gift of healing that he did not require
a face-to-face confrontation with his servant
whom Jesus said He had healed.
"And the servant was healed at that very moment,"
but the centurion had no proof of this until later.

This is what faith is all about—taking God at His word.
It all points up some serious flaws in my relationship
to the miracle-working God.
I ask—but don't receive what God offers.
I hear His promises, His word of deliverance,
His guarantee of life everlasting—
but am fearful of acting on them.
And then I wonder why my life is often a fruitless,
poverty-stricken kind of existence.
God is indeed great, and He is waiting to do great things
within me and through me among the unhappy, powerless,
hung-up people about me.

God help me to embrace Him,
    and His power and grace for daily living and serving,
    and begin to live and act like the royal, commissioned,
    empowered, and enabled son and servant
    that I am redeemed and assigned to be.

From Vision to Valley

Matthew 17:1-8

A mountain played an important role in the life of Jesus—
　　and especially in the lives of three of His disciples.
They, with Jesus, left the valley of human conflict
　　and frustration for a brief retreat on the heights
　　　　of a mountaintop.
Twelve men had left behind jobs, homes, families
　　to follow Christ.
They did so because they sensed something kingly
　　and authoritative about this son of a carpenter.
They marveled at His profound speeches;
　　they were amazed by His miracles,
　　held spellbound by His personality,
　　and were at one time or another convinced that He was
　　Israel's future king and they His right-hand men.
But it wasn't turning out that way.
Jesus appeared to be no closer to earthly power and glory
　　than He did following His baptism in the Jordan River.
They were beginning to have second thoughts,
　　especially when their Lord began making
　　some strange predictions about the terrible suffering
　　and eventual death He was soon to endure
　　at the hands of the respected religious leaders
　　who were already publicizing their animosity toward Him.
These following few were traversing valleys of despondency
　　and discouragement in those days.

They were in need of some special grace,
　　some further revelation
　　to shore up their failing hearts
　　and put new courage into their bones.
They needed a vision.

Perhaps it was in view
　　of their present doubts and depression,
　　and in view of the fierce trial by fire

they would experience in future months and years,
that three of these disciples
were permitted such a vision.
Why these three—James, John, and Peter?

It may be that James would need
the recollection of that scene
to cool his intolerant spirit, temper his ambition,
comfort him in Gethsemane, and nerve his faith
as he laid his head on Herod's block.
It might be the recollection of this significant vision
that would keep John from fleeing in haste
at Jesus' betrayal and give him the strength
to bear the sight of Christ's crucifixion.
Peter may have needed the memory of that vision
to strengthen his wavering courage,
to enable him to stand up against persecution
and press home to the consciences of his fellow beings
the claims of the crucified Lord,
to comfort other believers in trial,
and to testify to millions throughout history
that he was an eyewitness to Christ's majesty
and had heard with his own ears the voice from heaven
saying concerning this Christ:
"This is my beloved Son, with whom I am well pleased."

Thus three men, with Jesus, ascended a mountain.
According to Luke's Gospel,
they went up for the purpose of praying.
They received far more than they had bargained for.
"And He was transfigured before them . . .
a bright cloud overshadowed them,
and a voice from the cloud said,
'This is My beloved Son, with whom I am well pleased;
listen to Him.'"
It was a majestic, out-of-this world vision.
And in the midst of this transfiguration of the Christ
these disciples actually saw the prophets of old,
Moses and Elijah, talking with their Lord.
Peter was so ecstatic that he immediately wanted

to set up shrines for these three figures
    within the vision.

As significant as it was, this was only one incident
    in Christ's ministry
and a very small part
    of its total scheme and purpose.
Nevertheless, the vision on the mount taught the disciples
    and the church that followed in their wake
    some very important truths.
These truths were important to the disciples
    in view of what they would face
    in their immediate future.
They are no less important to me
    amidst the valley experiences
        of my temporal existence.

For one thing, *the transfigured Christ provided*
    a prophetic picture of the glory in which Christ
    and His followers will ultimately appear.
It was a brief glimpse into the dimension
    of the spiritual and the eternal.
Though the disciples may not
        have realized this at the moment,
        it was designed to alert them to the fact
        that they were destined for something far better
            than this earthly sojourn,
        that Christ's kingdom was not to be centered
        upon this globe nor in this time-and-space concept
            that I call life,
    that eternal reality is something which can never
    be comprehended by the finite faculties of humankind.
These disciples were at this time
    still on the other side of Easter,
    but what might this vision mean to me today?
It means that there is a victorious conclusion
    to this valley experience that is my present lot,
    even this conflict in which I am presently engaged.
It means that there is purpose and meaning
        to my daily plodding,

that the shadows of this life will serve
  to enhance the beauty of that which is to come.
It means that I need not place so much emphasis
  on temporal values,
    that poverty or failure here, though uncomfortable,
    is not tragic,
  that affliction in this life, though painful,
    does not have to be bitter and incapacitating.

Secondly, *the vision on the mount gives substance*
  to Jesus' teaching about the resurrection of the body
    and of life after death.
Over fourteen hundred years have elapsed since Moses died,
  and nine hundred years since Elijah was whisked off
    to heaven in a whirlwind.
  yet here they are seen alive by the three disciples.
Whatever it might have meant to them,
  it certainly ought to take the fear out of death
  for me and my Christian brothers and sisters.
It ought, as well, to remove the sorry sting
  of death's ravages in respect to our loved ones
    who have passed from us.
The vision before me is designed to encourage me,
    as it did the disciples,
  by bringing within range
  of the eye and the ear
    a glimpse of the hereafter.

Thirdly, *the transfiguration of Christ is testimony*
  and proof concerning the divinity of Christ.
Jesus was no eccentric philosopher
  or rabid, would-be king
    whom these disciples had left all to follow;
  He was God incarnate, God's Son,
    through whom He revealed Himself
    to the inhabitants of this planet.
I do well to gaze upon the transfigured Christ—
  and remember Him.
This is the Christ, the Son of God,
  and His promises to me—

promises of love, forgiveness,
   comfort, deliverance, eternal life—
are the promises of God Himself.
They are promises I can depend on
   in my valley experiences.
"This is My Son, My Chosen; listen to Him!"
   spoke the voice from heaven.

The verses following this Gospel lesson tell what happened
   when Jesus and the disciples came down from the mountain.
They were confronted with an epileptic boy
   down in the valley.
Jesus healed the boy and then proceeded on to Jerusalem,
   where He was to face trial and execution.

There are mountaintop experiences for me, too.
It may be a worship service, a weekend retreat,
   a meeting with friends, a period of meditation.
How often I have wanted to stay on the mountaintop,
   to build religious shrines, or to abide forever
   within the ecstasy of those precious hours!
It is, however, not meant to be
They are to prepare me for service in the valley.
There is where I am to labor in love for my Lord,
   here among the conflicts and contradictions,
   the fears and frustrations,
   the tragedies and heartaches,
   that abound in the valley.
It is here that I am to communicate,
   through my love for people,
   the love of an ever-loving God,
   and the vision of the eternal kingdom
   He has prepared for those who respond to His love.

The Press of Circumstance

Matthew 8:23-27

One's relationships to life are generally summed up
  in terms of relationships to God,
  fellow beings, possessions, and circumstances.
It is probably the last relationship that,
  interrelated with the others as it is,
  most often drives people into happiness or despair,
  optimism or depression—
  and in this kind of world usually resolves in pessimism
  because the circumstances that surround humankind
    are essentially tragic.
Most people are driven by their circumstances.
Some are driven or led to faith
  in God as revealed through Christ,
  or to some lesser religious philosophy,
  through their circumstances.
Then there are those, probably a much smaller group,
  who eventually learn how to stand above and beyond
  and even to master most of their circumstances.

It appears that many people lean continually
    with the wind of circumstance,
  no matter from which direction it blows.
They go with the stream,
  yield to the pressures about them.
They hinge their lives on events, like children living
  from one ice-cream cone to another
  or from one picnic to the next.
Vacation, shopping tour, visit with friends, payday,
  holiday, anniversary, beer-with-the-boys, bridge games,
  dinner out, dance, or a party—
  when the event is over, something dies,
  and they set their sights on the next event
    that hovers on the horizon.

30

This is still the experience of many
    who call themselves Christian—
    and this in spite of that great Event,
    the incarnation, the redemption of humankind
        made possible through Christ,
    which should become the eternal focus
    of their lives and keep them continually
        within divine purposes and objectives.
It is almost always the experience of the pagan,
    the nonbeliever, who has made this temporal world
        his or her absolute
    and who kowtows at the altar
        of materialism and sensualism.
For such a person to insist,
    that he is running his own life,
    or that she is the master of her own fate,
    is as futile as a dog barking at the moon.
The wind of circumstance, be it joyous or unhappy,
    success or failure, pain or pleasure,
    will likely lead and drive such people,
    as surely as a horse is led and driven
        by bit and bridle and whip.
To these people life is more or less a sort of gamble.
They keep hoping for "breaks."
One's luck, or fate, is either good or bad.
Some have been endowed with more brains than others;
    some with specific talents and abilities.
Some are never sick; others are afflicted for life.
It would appear that most people
    are driven by circumstance,
    and whether they be happy or miserable
    depends upon the circumstances
    that press about their daily lives.

There are, of course, those who are driven to Christ,
    apparently by means of the circumstances about them.
It is probable that the circumstances of life
    have an important part to play
    in most conversions to the Christian faith.

Even the sturdy fishermen of Galilee
   were thoroughly frightened
   by the violent storm that beset their little boat.
"Save, Lord; we are perishing,"
   they cried out to their Lord, who was asleep.
The ugly circumstances of the executioner's cross
   opened the heart of one of the thieves
   to the loving grace of God.
"Jesus, remember me when you come into Your kingdom,"
   he cried out in the final hours of his life.
I don't believe that God inflicts pain and tragedy
   upon His creatures.
It is part and parcel of this fractured world
   in which I live.
There is no doubt, however, that the Spirit of God
   is active even amidst the painful
   and undesirable episodes of people's lives.
I'll never forget how my mother
   sometimes had to take away my toys,
   or call me from romping with my playmates,
   only to set me before the piano and make me go through
   a rugged hour of scales and finger exercises.
God, through the wind of circumstance, often allows
   the snatching away of the toys of men and women,
   even their health, jobs, incomes, possessions,
   those things they loved above all else,
   in order that they might face up to the reality
      of God Himself,
   and their personal relationship with Him.
To be driven to Christ or encouraged to turn to God
      through the wind of circumstance
   is by no means a cowardly or shameful thing.
Even this is made possible
   only by the power of God's Spirit.
Whereas the maze of life on this earth
   is tragedy and despair, Christ is the only way out.
It is, at times, only when this despair
      induced by circumstances
   points to Him that many people find this way out.

There is then that much smaller groups of people
   who eventually learn how to live
   over and beyond the power and influence
   of circumstances in their lives.

They even learn
   how to master and drive their circumstances,
   transforming them into vehicles of blessing
   for their lives and the lives of others about them.
I note in other Gospel lessons how Jesus had power
   over the circumstances of disease.
In this Gospel lesson He is shown to have power
   over the forces of nature.
In other words,
   there is no circumstance or set of circumstances
   over which Christ is not all-powerful.
Even the disciples had not yet reached this stage of faith
   in their relationship to the Christ.
If they had, they would not have become panic stricken
   during the storm on the lake.
They would have known
   that their Lord would awaken when necessary,
   that God is never asleep to the needs of His children.
"Why are you afraid, O men of little faith?"
"Why are you such cowards?" Jesus may be saying
   to many of His followers today.
"How little faith you have!
I have created, redeemed, and appointed you
   for just such times as these.
I am always with you, indwelling you, empowering you,
   working out My will through you.
You don't have to be afraid.
Trust Me; I won't let you go.
There is a quiet harbor
   somewhere at the end of your journey,
   but for now you are to abide in Me
   and work for Me in the midst of the storm."

It is one thing, and it is no small thing,
   to be driven to Christ through the weight and pressure

of difficult circumstances in my life.
It is quite another to so confide in my Lord,
   to so trust and love Him,
   that I can embrace my circumstances,
   no matter how difficult they may seem to be,
   to accept them as coming
   by way of God's permissive will
   and designed to accomplish some purpose in my life,
   even to accept them as gifts of God,
   a measure of His love and mercy.
This was Paul's attitude in the midst of his trials
   and tribulations: "Give thanks in all circumstances,
   for this is the will of God in Christ Jesus for you . . .
   Always and for everything giving thanks in the name
   of our Lord Jesus Christ to God the Father."

"Then [Jesus] rose and rebuked the winds and the sea;
   and there was a great calm."
I would like to be one of that small group of followers
   who, filled with God's Spirit,
   dare to do what Jesus did—
   rise up and rebuke their circumstances—
   those circumstances, particularly,
   that threaten human dignity and freedom,
   which perpetrate war and promote class hatred,
   the circumstances of injustice, oppression, racism—
   much of this too often the consequence
   of my own apathy and self-centeredness.

The same Spirit who impelled and empowered Jesus Christ
   is supposed to be empowering and impelling me
   who claim His name.
It is high time I begin to act
   like the Christian I claim to be
   and, at the risk of property, reputation, or life itself,
   rise up to rebuke the forces of evil
      and the circumstances they generate
   and dedicate myself anew
      to God's purposes for me and my society.

Crossing Out the Cross

Matthew 4:1-11

The glories of the Epiphany season are now behind me.
It was an exciting time—
  being witness to a series of manifestations
  of Jesus' majesty in His baptism, His miracles,
  His revelation of Himself as the Messiah,
  His transfiguration on the mount.
These added up to some heady, hearty experiences.

Now I must come back to earth again,
  back to my three-dimensional world,
  to the sufferings and conflicts
    that plague this planet.
I am now introduced to the season of Lent.
While the Lenten Gospel lessons point me to and prepare me
  for the high festival of Easter,
  they lead me, as well, into considering
  some very serious things
  about my nature and my world
  that highlight the Easter event
  as the crown and apex of the church year.
Words like sin, death, temptation, repentance, Satan,
  cross, burial, break into my contemplations.

The Gospel lesson pictures a dramatic struggle.
It is, of all things, a contest
  between Christ, God's beloved Son,
  and Satan, the personification of all the evil forces
  that permeate the world and afflict its inhabitants.
The stakes are high.
The winner will take all.
The fact that I already know the outcome of the drama
  makes the event of no less importance to me.
I need its reassurance in my own battles against
  the designs and purposes of the evil one.

The battle plans of the Christ will be found
    to be most effective in my hours of temptation.

To prepare Himself
    for what was now to be His public ministry
    in the valley of humanity's problems and conflicts,
    Jesus went on a forty-day retreat
    for the purpose of fasting, praying, and meditating.
It was here that He was to consider
    the principles and methods of fulfilling
    His destiny among men and women.
And it was here that He was confronted by Satan—
    by temptations to compromise or take shortcuts
    in the accomplishment of His Father's purposes.
The first temptation of Jesus appears to focus primarily
    upon His human needs.
It was to a very hungry Christ that the devil suggested:
    "If you are [really] the Son of God,
    command these stones to become loaves of bread."
It is an ever-recurring temptation in my life.
There are, even within the silence
    of my devout contemplations,
    those insidious whispers of my human nature
    that fill my heart and mind
    with fleshly and materialistic concerns.
There is, in the crush of material demands,
    the temptation to relegate God to the background.
It is not the crass choice between God and bread;
    one may even combine the two with some degree of piety.
The tragic fact is that, all too often,
    God ends up in second place in my life.

Jesus would not yield to the temptation
    of using His divine powers
    to satisfy His own human needs.
He had entered into the human conflict;
    He must accept the human condition of His incarnation.
He recognized that man and woman
    cannot "live by bread alone."
They must be fed.

Social justice must be preached.
Economic problems must be solved.
The far greater need of humankind, however,
   involves the spiritual and the eternal.
It is a person's relationship to God, the Father,
   that gives that person his distinctive character.
Apart from that relationship,
   the human being can only be owned
      by the things about him.

Seeing that Jesus refused to subscribe to the belief
      that the human creature is all stomach,
      the devil took Jesus to the Holy City and set Him
      on the pinnacle of the temple.
"If you are the Son of God, throw yourself down;
   for it is written,
   'He will give His angels charge of you' and
   'On their hands they will bear you up,
   lest you strike your foot against a stone.'"
This, *the second temptation,* might well be verbalized:
   "Why take the long and bitter way
   to win Yourself a following
   through being despised and rejected—
   even through the shedding of your blood?
   If you are God, pick your own course.
   Do something spectacular, heroic, fantastic.
   You'll have a crowd at Your feet in no time.
   Be a magician; clothe Yourself with wonders.
   It is the spectacular that people want, not the divine.
   Do something striking and breathtaking,
   but leave their guilty consciences alone."

The temptation is ever present within the church today.
The elaborate programs, the complex organizations,
   the colorful ceremonies, theater-like productions,
   bright, gifted personalities, the emotional splurges,
   the exciting entertainment
      presented in the name of religion—
   all indicate it to be a temptation often yielded to.

So, too, in my private life, the spiritual forces
  of evil and darkness would ever be satisfied with
    "form without power."
"Just put on a good show;
  go through the motions of being religious,"
    they would say to me,
  "but don't let it alter your personal life too much."

Then the devil took Jesus to a high mountain
  and showed Him all the kingdoms of the world.
"All these I will give You," he said,
  "if you will fall down and worship me."
In this, *the third temptation*, Satan may be saying:
  "You have come, O Christ, to win the world,
  but the world is mine. I will give it to You
  if You will compromise a little
  and pay allegiance to me—
  or at least coexist with me.
  Forget the cross. Here's the world at your feet—
  loud hosannas, shiny crowns, adoring crowds—
  and all this without thorns or nails."

I doubt that the devil had much hope
  of tripping up the Christ
  with this extremely base temptation,
  but this was truly the incarnate Christ,
  with all the weaknesses of the human flesh,
  so the evil one could do no less than try.
Unfortunately, I have fallen for it at times.
When applied to earthly mortals, it may be the temptation
  to reduce God to something they can handle,
  to conform Him to some earthly image
  or to one that people can worship
  without discomfort or sacrifice, problem or pain.
I wonder if I, in effect,
  am challenging God to prove Himself,
  to show me a flash of power,
  to make Himself available at my command,
  insisting that He always be responsive
  to my assumed needs.

The entire period of temptation in the life of Christ
  may be summed up as the devil's attempt to cross out
  the cross in the ministry of Jesus.
Had he succeeded in doing that,
  salvation would not have been made available
    for humankind;
  sin would not have been atoned for;
  the kingdom of God would not include creatures
    from this planet,
  and the spiritual forces of evil,
    would have won the day.
Jesus, however, did not fall
  for these insidious temptations.
He set His face toward Jerusalem,
  placing the cross at the very center of His plan
    for humanity's salvation,
  and it was there that He demonstrated
    and made available and applicable
  God's forgiving and sanctifying love
    for every man and woman.

While the devil failed in his temptations of the Christ,
  he still hopes to succeed in his persistent attempts
  to detour me from the road that leads to the cross—
  to cross out the cross in my relationship to God.
In order to resist his temptations,
  and this only by the grace of God,
  I must not only accept God's grace
    and the forgiveness of sin
  that comes by way of the cross
    Jesus ascended on my behalf;
  I must yield to Christ's injunction to carry my cross,
  to endure whatever sacrifice or suffering
    may come my way,
  in order that my brothers and sisters about me
  may be led to embrace that saving grace of God
  that is offered to them by way of the cross of Christ.

The spiritual forces of darkness
  will continue to afflict and tempt me.

41

And I will not always succeed in resisting temptation.
The efforts of those dark forces will, however, be in vain
   as long as I allow the cross of Christ to infiltrate
   and influence every phase of my being—
   and resolve to bear my own cross
   in obedience to Him and in love for my fellow persons.

Why Is God So Stubborn?

Matthew 15:21-28

Why is God so stubborn?
It is a question I have asked at one time or another.
There are times when I have felt that God
    is downright obstinate and seems to be cold,
    indifferent, unrelated to my aches and agonies.
He not only allows me to get into complexities
    and entanglements that I really have no intention
        or desire to get into,
    but He seems at times to be totally oblivious
        to my struggles and conflicts.

I have faced this frustrating circumstance in my own life.
I have met up with it again and again in the lives
        of those I have counseled:
    an alcoholic sincerely wants deliverance
    but is compulsively held fast by the demon rum;
    a wife, or a husband, is prostrate with grief
    because the spouse for no apparent reason wants out
        or files for divorce;
    a breadwinner suddenly loses his job
    and has no one to turn to for financial help;
    a beautiful child is snatched from adoring parents
    through sickness or accident;
    a father leaves behind dependent mother and children
    by taking his own life.
I agree that God is in His heaven—
    lest I be accused of blasphemy or heresy—
    but there are occasions when He plainly appears
    to have abdicated this chaotic world.
Though I can hardly blame Him for that,
    I certainly wish He would stick around
    and throw some light on my dark problems.

When I am cornered, I realize, of course,
  that this inability to get through to God,
  this apparent lack of communication,
  is basically my inability, my lack.
Lost in the fog of my besetting sins and failures,
  I am incapable of hearing His voice
  or sensing His direction for my life.
Nevertheless, there are times when I sincerely
  want His deliverance and seek His will.
I want to be set free from my weaknesses;
  I want answers to my problems;
  I want light on my obscure path.
He miraculously demonstrated such deliverances in His
  walk upon the earth, manifesting His divine power—
  even to the extent of raising people from the dead.
It is difficult to interpret His contemporary reluctance
  to do the same for me
  except as stubbornness or obstinacy.

It may be that the incident of this Gospel lesson
  will throw some light
    on the problem of an obstinate God.
While Jesus was walking with His disciples
    beyond the boundaries of Israel
He was approached by a woman with a mentally deranged
    or demon-possessed daughter.
Jesus heeded not her cry for help
    and continued on His course.
She would not be repulsed and continued to follow Him
    until He and His disciples reached their destination.
She knelt at Jesus' feet crying, "Lord, have mercy."
Her persistence prevailed.
"O woman!" Jesus said, "great is your faith!
Be it done for you as you desire."
She went home and found her daughter delivered
    from her sickness.

In view of this incident, what must I do
    to press the miracle-working God
        to act on my behalf?

It is obvious that *my need must be desperate.*
I must want His deliverance from my dilemma,
   His answer to my problem,
   His light in my darkness
      with all my heart.
"Do you want to be healed?"
   was Jesus' first question to the man
   who had been crippled for thirty-eight years.
This is half the battle—
   to want help, to need desperately.
In my relationship to God it must be a need
   for *His* deliverance, *His* answer, *His* healing.
And if I am as desperate for deliverance
      as was the Canaanite woman,
   I am not going to be concerned about *how* God gives it,
      only the fact that He can and will.

My pursuit must be persistent.
Jesus enjoined His listeners to "ask . . . seek . . . knock . . .
   and it will be given you."
He suggests, thereby, that I be persistent
   in my heaven-directed requests.
At another time Jesus spoke of a widow who went
   to a judge to seek vindication over her enemies.
The judge refused at first,
   but because of her persistence
   finally granted her request.
Jesus isn't affirming that God is stubborn,
   but is indicating that I must be intense enough
   about my pursuit to be persistent.
It may be that this is necessary
   in order to prepare myself
   for God's answer or response.

My faith must be intense
"O woman, great is your faith!" Jesus exclaimed.
He who was so discouraged about the rebellious unbelief
   of His own people was profoundly impressed
   by the obvious faith of this foreigner.

Even faith, the ability to trust and believe in God,
    is a heaven-sent gift.
It is one, however, that is either lost and destroyed
    or strengthened and enlarged by the struggle
    and tussle of one's daily conflicts.
Self-confidence is a necessary ingredient
        in all human success and happiness,
        but total self-reliance is disaster-bound
        and resolves in defeat.
My prime battle in this life
    is with the supernatural forces of darkness.
There I can fight effectively only with the use
    of God-given, supernatural weapons
    and when endowed by supernatural power.
God does not give real answers
    to flippant and halfhearted prayers
    because He is not an automat or vending machine.
He is God, my God,
    and only when I truly rely on Him as such
    can I expect a response from Him.

My attitude must be one of patience.
Even though the Canaanite woman saw no tangible evidence
        of divine deliverance,
    she eagerly turned down the homeward path
    convinced that Christ had worked a miracle
        of healing and deliverance.
God does not deliver on demand.
More often than not His deliverance is a process
    which takes place over a period of time,
    and often with the assistance of human instruments
    who may be unknowingly participating
        in that deliverance.
He may withhold the miracle of deliverance because I am
    not ready to receive it, or because of some purpose
    a particular affliction
        is destined to serve in my life.
Or His miracle-working power may already be at work
    in my life and I don't even recognize it.

47

It is possible, as well, that He is gradually bringing me
to that point where I, myself, by His enabling grace
can bring about the very deliverance I prayed for.

My surrender must be total.
"For this is the will of God, your sanctification,"
wrote the apostle Paul.
When I go to a doctor, he listens patiently
to my complaints about nosebleeding or heartburn
and then proceeds to examine me from head to toe.
A dentist considers the aching tooth I point out
and then proceeds to find a half-dozen or so
other teeth that need immediate attention.
Paul is saying, in effect, that God
does not primarily will the eradication
of my specifc problems or affliction,
but the consecration of my total life to Him.
He may or may not remove the affliction,
but what is more important, He seeks to captivate
and possess the total person with and for Himself.
Thus the answer to my problem,
the fulfilling of my need,
the deliverance from my dilemma,
can be expected only if I consecrate and commit
my whole life to God and His purposes.

Why is God so stubborn?
It is because He loves me so much that He insists
on giving me the very best in life.
The only way He has of introducing me to the best
is to sometimes allow me to prick myself
on the thorny bushes of this existence,
or run amok in its blind alleys and dead-end streets,
or flail helplessly in its quicksands
of ultimate disillusionment and disaster.
When I desperately long for deliverance,
I have already taken the first step.
That miracle of deliverance will be performed,
or the miracle of sufficient grace
to bear my affliction

or to live fruitfully and effectively
    with my problem,
when I yield the reins of my life
to my loving God and Father
and discover in this relationship
    eternal grace and joy.
It is not enough that I bring my problem to God.
I must bring myself to Him,
    with all that I am and have.
Then miracles will happen in my life,
    and above all, the miracle of my redemption
    and my adoption into the eternal family of God.

The Lord Does Provide

John 6:1-15

In Lewis Carroll's *Through the Looking Glass,*
  Alice in Wonderland meets the White Knight.
He is quite a sight to behold.
He is cumbered with contraptions.
They include a beehive to capture a vagrant swarm of bees,
  a mousetrap to make short work of molesting rodents,
  anklets around his horse's feet
    to protect it against sharks,
  and a dish in anticipation of the plum pudding
    some kind soul might offer him.
Laden with gadgets, this White Knight might well be a symbol
  of misguided people who seek happiness
    by accumulating things.
While this White Knight looks ridiculous,
  I wonder what I and my friends look like
  to some angel from the celestial world
  who somehow got off course and landed on this earth.
He would see all sorts of White Knights
    cumbered with gadgets:
  cars, boats, wardrobes, furniture, sports equipment,
  antique collections, hobby corners, inherited collections
  of who knows what from generations back.
There are rugs on the floors, pictures on the walls,
  assorted articles on the shelves,
  and machines to wash, dry, vacuum,
  cool, heat, freeze, cook, entertain—
  all of them designed to please, comfort,
    titillate, and tantalize
  the five senses each human was created with.
If angels ever get sick, they would surely
  laugh themselves sick at this clutter of things
  that earthly beings must utilize
  to keep themselves in motion.

While I hesitate to consider myself a White Knight,
   I must admit that I all too often
   interpret my personal needs
   in terms of some material lack,
   a need for some thing or things.
This is probably the greatest stumbling block
   to God's kingdom that I face,
   because it obscures my real need,
   which is met only in a relationship of love and trust
   in God my Creator and Christ my Savior.
There are people who stumble over this
   and never rise again.
They find enough happiness and contentment,
   or continually expect to,
   in the temporal values about them,
   and never discover the eternal joy
   of God's design and destiny for them.

One of Jesus' most striking miracles,
   particularly in view of the large number
   of individuals affected,
   is the feeding of the five thousand.
In some ways the miracle is a very strange one.
The religious leaders of Christ's day were concocting
   ways to get rid of Him.
On the other hand, there was a movement afoot,
   probably known and encouraged by the disciples,
   to compel Jesus to come forth and declare Himself
      as king of Israel.
Now, as if to accentuate His popularity
      and standing with the people,
   He performs this amazing miracle
   which could only serve to fire up their enthusiasm
   and intensify their desire to crown Him as their king.

If I were to conjecture about the meaning
   of this happening in the ministry of Jesus,
   I would guess that it pointed up Christ's *concern*
for these people who had gathered to see and hear Him.
He was concerned

about the physical needs and desires of humanity.
It wasn't essential that He feed this multitude before Him.
It was not a matter of their starving;
    they could have procured food at neighboring villages.
Yet Jesus took special care,
        drawing on supernatural power and provision,
        to feed this mass of people who had been following Him
        and hanging on His every word.
Not only is God concerned about the needs of His children,
    He is able to meet them—whatever they may be.

The Lord will provide.
This is not a trite phrase; it is eternal truth
    which I and my fellow Christians have experienced
        over and over again.
It is God's desire that I continue to rely on His promises,
    to demonstrate the audacity of faith
        that expects great things
    though there be nothing visible
        upon which to build.
This is far more reliable than creeping common sense
    that adheres to facts which are mere shadows
    and forgets the chief fact that I have
    an almighty God and Father, Helper, Friend at my side
    who is at all times concerned about my material needs.

Jesus is concerned
    about the material needs of His followers,
    but this is not His primary concern.
Amazed by this astounding feat,
    the people attempted to force Him
        into becoming their king.
Just think, a king who would and could
        keep them free and fed
    no matter what the condition
        of the world or the weather!
Jesus had to run for the hills to get away from them.
Some of the people caught up with Him the following day.
Their first request was:
    "Lord, give us this bread always."

The Lord's response to these shallow inquirers—
and to their fellow travelers who claim His name today:
"I am the bread of life;
he who comes to Me shall not hunger,
and he who believes in Me shall never thirst."
Thus Christ's concern resolved into a deep *conviction*
and the resultant proclamation that the real need
of God's creatures was their need for God,
and that they could find God
by accepting and believing in this Christ.
This was the purpose of His coming to them—
not to be their earthly king and continue to pamper
their physical needs,
but to give His life as a ransom,
to ascend the cross on their behalf,
to conquer over sin and death and make eternal life
a possibility for all of humankind
and thereby assure the everlasting satisfaction
of all people's needs and wants.
The author of our Gospel lesson later reveals the response
to Jesus' answer and conviction
concerning His ministry to them:
"After this many of His disciples drew back
and no longer went about with Him."

The miracle which reveals Jesus' concern and conviction
for God's creatures also pictures and presents
a tremendous *commission*.
For one thing,
it portrays the desperate need of the world.
The hungry multitude about Christ represented need,
the thing most common to every human being.
There are hundreds of millions on this planet
who are in need of the most fundamental elements
of physical existence—
food, clothing, medicine, shelter, security, freedom.
There is within all of humanity the need
for inner assurance and serenity,
for meaning and purpose in life.

The miracle in question portrays the mighty,
    eternally sufficient provision of God.
"Jesus then took the loaves, and when He had given thanks,
    He distributed them to those who were seated;
    so also with the fish, as much as they wanted."
A miracle to thrill them and bread to fill them—
    what a day it must have been!
And all this time Christ's real purpose
    was to convince these people
    that He who could miraculously and supernaturally satisfy
    the pangs of their physical hunger
    could also fulfill
    the inner desires and needs of their hearts.

Between the famished five thousand
    and heaven's supernatural provision
    was a little boy with five barley loaves and two fish.
He brought a lunch with him on this exciting day.
Then he did a selfless, generous thing.
He offered them to Jesus to do with as He would.
It was a profoundly significant and sacrificial act,
    for it is here, in this simple little incident,
    that I come across something of the meaning
        of the cross
    and my commission as a follower of Jesus Christ.
The bridge between God's abundant provision
    and the world's desperate need
    is the sacrificial love-offering.
It was first made by God Himself, who through Christ
    descended from His throne of glory,
    stooped to the humiliating level of man's sin,
    took upon Himself humanity's guilt,
    and suffered the wages of sin on its behalf.
The lad gave all he had,
    and Jesus blessed this tiny gift
    and fed five thousand hungry bodies.

Today I, as an individual and a member of Christ's body,
    the church, stand as God's representative and agent

between the world's desperate needs
   and heaven's abundant provision.
This is my commission, and God holds me,
   along with the church at large,
   responsible for channeling His eternal grace and gifts
   to those who are in need.
I may appear to be and often feel myself to be
   as insignificant as the little boy
      with his fish and buns,
   but I am not insignificant to God,
   and by His grace will become a channel and communicator
   of His life and love to my fellow persons about me.

Coming to Terms—with Death

John 8:46-59

After Xerxes, the Persian king,
   marching with his immense army to invade Greece,
   arrived at the Hellespont,
   he ordered a grand review of his troops.
A throne was set up for him on the hillside,
   and seating himself upon that marble chair
   he surveyed his million soldiers in the fields below.
With a proud smile he turned to his courtiers
   and stated that he was the happiest man on earth.
Then his countenance changed, and those men near to him
   saw the tears begin to trickle down his cheeks.
One of the group asked the cause
   of this strange and unreasonable grief.
"Alas!" said Xerxes,
   "I am thinking that of all this vast host,
   not one will be alive in a hundred years."

It seems strange that the last thing
   that most human beings are willing
     to come to terms with
   is the very thing
     that is most certain to take place.
I refer to the phenomenon of death.
One is reminded of it almost every day of his life.
I still remember fanning myself
   in Middle West rural churches
   with fans provided by the local mortuary.
They were often imprinted
   with some touching word of comfort
   like "We've never turned anyone away."
Almost everyone retains scar-tissue memories of the cold,
   grossly made-up faces of loved ones
   confined to long boxes banked with flowers.

I'll never forget the cold winds
    and the sickening thuds of frozen mud-clods
    shoveled into fresh graves
    on the Dakota prairies.
Even if I could forget the past,
    there are always fresh reminders,
    and often ugly reminders. . . .

"Any man's death diminishes me,
    because I am involved in mankind,"
        wrote John Donne,
    "and therefore never send to know
    for whom the bell tolls;
    it tolls for thee."
"It is appointed for men to die once,
    and after that comes judgment,"
        proclaims the New Testament.
"So teach us to number our days
    that we may get a heart of wisdom,"
        said the psalmist.
Everyone meets death—in one way or another.
Some meet it grandly, a speech in hand.
Some talk about it as if going to a long-delayed banquet.
Some sputter in the face of death like a wet fuse.
Some are impatient and belligerent; others are bewildered.
Some are stoic and attempt to be philosophical about it.
There is dignity and grace in the death of some;
    there is fear, even terror, for others.
I have been with many people on the threshold
    of this unknown journey that they must take alone.
I have found again and again, that those who face it,
    not always without fear and misapprehension,
    but with courage bathed in hope,
    are those who have come to terms with it
    and who have found in the Christian faith
    a meaning and purpose in the prospect of death.

The Gospel lesson reveals the reason
    that the Christian faith alone
    has the answer to the phenomenon of death,

and why this faith offers something no philosophy
or religion can begin to offer,
a hope and a promise that will all but obliterate
the fear of death.
It is emphatically expressed in the words of Jesus:
"Truly, truly, I say to you, if anyone keeps My Word,
he will never see death."
In a few concise words He addresses Himself
to the greatest and most profound contradiction
of the Christian life:
that whereas everyone shall die,
there is no real death
for those who are in Christ Jesus.
"I am the resurrection and the life," He said
in the eleventh chapter of John's Gospel;
"he who believes in Me,
though he die, yet shall he live,
and whoever lives and believes in Me
shall never die."
"For the love of Christ controls us,"
wrote the apostle Paul,
"because we are convinced that one has died for all;
therefore all have died."
And to Timothy, Paul wrote about this Christ
"who abolished death and brought life
and immortality to light through the Gospel."

Every man must die for himself,
but this is only the first death,
the discarding of this mortality,
the putting off of these human garments
with all the pains and sufferings,
weaknesses and frustrations.
The second death,
that eternal death that perpetually destroys,
no man or woman need experience.
This death has been substituted for—
by the death of Jesus Christ.
Because He died and rose from the dead,

no one needs to die the second death.
I can face death without fear because I have
   the hope of life after death.
I shall live again, joyfully, eternally, purposefully,
   unrestrained by the contradictions and conflicts
   which beset this mortal life.
Thus death for a Christian
   is not an ugly, atrocious thing,
   though the manner in which some people die
   is most certainly so.
It is not something to contemplate with horror.
   It is the carrying on of the grand adventures of life,
   of which death is a part.
It is in reality a process of *becoming*.
   and is as important a part of that process
      as life itself.
I have divinely instilled within me
   the urge for totality, completeness, perfection.
This calls for a growth and development
   which comes only at the price of death.
"If anyone keeps My Word, he will never see death,"
   said Jesus.
He will see only life, the total goal, the completeness
   upon which life has been focused even from birth.

"My life is a mystery," someone has said,
   "but death is a dark malady which faith cannot evade.
Yet faith has a word; it speaks of process and purpose,
   of which death is a part,
   and it speaks of something steady
   over all the wreckage."
I cannot entirely ignore the ugliness of death,
   nor minimize its horror.
I cannot forget my first childhood contact with it,
   nor the shock and pain of its brutal invasion
   of my family circle.
Despite the poets' attempts to picture it
   as nothing more than a sweet slumber,
   the philosophers and their explanations,

the preachers and their promises,
   there is a horror about death that strikes fear
      into my heart.
I cannot completely rid myself of its insidious threat
   to my being—at least not yet.
As surely as comes the end of summer,
   so surely must I face up to the fact of death,
   its parting of the ways,
   its incomprehensible darkness.

"Yet faith has a word,"
   an answer for this ultimate anxiety.
Christ not only faced it, bluntly and biologically;
   He was victorious over it.
He translated it from an enemy bent on my destruction
   into a friend that promises to usher me
      into eternal glory.
If this is true—
   and I believe with all my heart that it is—
   then even death can be beautiful.

King for a Day

Matthew 21:1-11

There were two parades in Jerusalem
  on that first Holy Week so long ago.
Both held the same figure as the center of attraction.
The first parade was one of exuberant welcome,
  with the shouting of "hosannas"
  and the waving of palm branches.
A few days later the attention of Jerusalem was focused
  upon a parade of another sort.
The central figure was the same;
  so were the shouting crowds—
  at least there very likely were some
  who took part in both parades.
Their cry, however, portrayed a different tone.
The cry of "hosannas" had turned
  into ominous proclamations of hate.
"Crucify Him, crucify Him," was the theme
    of this noisy throng.
There He was, the same Christ,
  bruised, bleeding, bending
  under the burden of a heavy cross.
Surrounded by soldiers with bared swords,
  executioners with cracking whips were driving
    this pathetic figure
  to that infamous spot where the cross He bore
  would in turn bear Him in torturous agony.

It is still difficult to believe that in five short days
  "hosannas" can turn to "crucify,"
  and exuberant crowds can become murdering tyrants.
Why? How can this be?

Knowing my own bigoted, prejudiced, two-faced nature,
  it is not too difficult for me to see
  the reason for this unsavory affair.

For one thing, this Jesus
    so gladly welcomed on Palm Sunday,
    coming in the name of the Messiah
    and in the manner of the ancient prophecies,
    refused to fit into the formula and concept
    of what those crowds expected this Christ to be.
"For I have come down from heaven," He once said,
    "not to do My own will,
    but the will of Him who sent Me."
In obedience to this will "He set His face"
    toward the course that would deliberately bypass
        the honor and esteem of people,
    a course which appeared to be oblivious
        to their superficial needs and wants—
    a course that twisted the acclaim of Palm Sunday
    into the mocking, murderous assault of Black Friday.
Another reason for this swift change of attitudes,
        between the two crowds
    is that the course Jesus chose involved
    His pointing out people's utter inability
    to keep the revered Law
    and to find salvation thereby.
He would not fit into their schemes;
    they would not accept His message or identify
        with His purposes.
He must go. "Crucify Him, crucify Him!"
Thus the rabid mob of Black Friday,
    the hideous cross, the intense suffering,
    and the darkest hour in the history of the world.

I wonder what would happen
    if Christ rode into my city today.
Of this one could be sure,
    the extravaganza that would accompany such a happening
    would make that event in Jerusalem
    look like a family picnic.
I doubt that He would be permitted to ride a donkey.
There would be limousines and police escorts,
    bands and floats.

City dignitaries would spare neither trouble nor expense
    to make it the most impressive,
    ever-to-be-remembered event
    in the history of the city.
The populace, most of whom
    have not attended a church for the past year,
    would line the streets to throw confetti
    and scream out their "hosannas" or "hurrahs."
He would be given the key to the city,
    showered with gifts, and put up in the finest hotel.
Churches would probably be lost
    in the shuffle of grandeur and display
    demonstrated by the political and business
        endeavors of the city.
No church, certainly, would be large enough to hold
    the crowds that would gather to hear Him speak.

Then, perhaps, the tide would turn—
    and possibly for the same reasons that caused
    that turn of events in Jerusalem so long ago.
Somehow, this Divine One would not fit
    into the common connotations of Himself.
The long lines of malady-ridden
    would not all find healing.
The thousands who came to see miracles and signs
    might be disappointed.
They would hear from His lips
    that the things they had centered their lives upon
    were not really that important.
Instead of platitudes there might be pronouncements
    about human iniquity.
People would begin to see their own glaring sins
    in the blazing light of His righteousness—
    their apathy and self-centeredness,
    their bigotry and lovelessness,
    their love of possessions rather than love of people.
God's created children might not be able
    to withstand His pure, sacrificial, grace-giving love
        as revealed through this Jesus Christ,

or His injunctions to receive such love
and to identify with divine purposes
in communicating love to the world about them.
This Jesus and His invitation to follow Him
simply would not fit into their programs and agendas
in a competitive, profit-and-gain society
where people put themselves and their needs
above those of others.
It is impractical, unreasonable, even dangerous
in respect to all the human family holds dear.
Finding themselves stripped naked of all pretense
under the piercing eye of the all-seeing One,
people who refused to fall on their faces in repentance
would probably react in rebellion.
There might well be a parade of another sort—
this one leading out of the city.
It would not lead to execution hill;
the crowd would be too sophisticated for that.
There would, however, be multitudes who would find
some reason for turning their own feelings
of guilt and shame upon this loving Christ
and would cast Him in disgraceful rejection
out of their hearts, homes, and community.
From Palm Sunday to Black Friday—
it's not so strange after all.
It could happen even today.

Can it be expressed more graphically than in the words
of St. John Adcock?
"We want no living Christ,
Whose truth intense
Pretends to no belief
in our pretense
And, flashing on all
Folly and deceit,
Would blast our world
To ashes at our feet . . ."
The fact is, it does happen here—
it is happening here even now.

Christ *has* marched into my city.
He does not make a visible entrance as God in the flesh,
    but He has come, in part,
    through the established institutions of the church.
He proclaims His purposes
    and reveals His gift of salvation
        through the Word and the sacraments.
The pathetic truth is that only a few
    out of the great masses
    recognize Him, accept Him, honor and worship Him.
The great majority of people in my thriving community
    thrive and strive without Him or in spite of Him.
They have no inclination to crucify Him;
    they simply ignore Him.
They may on occasion,
    such as an annual Easter celebration,
    pay Him their sincere respects,
    and then politely pass Him by.

Christ has marched into my community, my church, my home.
He seeks to ascend the throne of my heart and life.
He has not come to judge and to punish me
    for my indifference, rebelliousness, or foolish neglect,
    my apparent inability, to see
    through the maze of materialism
    into my real heart needs.
He has come, rather, to bear the judgment for all this
    upon Himself.
This is the reason for Good Friday,
    and the meaning of the cross.
Before Easter can dawn, there must be a Good Friday;
    before the empty tomb there must be the cross.
Before I can share with the crucified Christ
    the resurrection and the glorious inheritance
        of life everlasting,
    I must come by way of that cross—
    not to ascend it, but to kneel before it
        in contrition and penitence,
    laying my sins upon Him,

accepting His great sacrifice on my behalf,
and crowning Him as Savior and King of my life.
It is only then that the Christ who marched into Jerusalem
   can march into my life,
   to inhabit my innermost being
   and make His presence known and felt
      in and through me—
   in my home, my church, and my community.

If I Really Believed

Mark 16:1-8

It appeared,
   in those hours following the burial of Jesus,
   that Christianity died with the Christ
   and was laid with Him in the sepulcher.
There was not a single human being who believed
   they would ever see Him again.
What remained for the disciples but to return
   to their homes and their fishing nets
   as disappointed and disillusioned men,
   and try their best to forget
   the whole amazing experience?
There never were men more utterly depressed and dispirited
   than were the disciples of Christ
   following His crucifixion.

Then something happened.
A few hours later, and these same men
   were full of confidence and joy.
Their faith in Jesus had revived,
   and Christianity had a far greater vitality
      than ever before.
The once defeated and disillusioned disciples
   now became men sent out for world conquest.
They who had once sought for thrones
   were now fearlessly expecting persecution and death.
Christ's death had cowed, discouraged, terrified,
   and defeated them.
Now they were virtually transfigured and transformed.
They were new men, ready to go boldly into the very city
   that had crucified their leader
   and proclaim Him as Savior of the world.
Ordinary, fallible, blundering men, they were changed
   from inferior failures into flaming messengers.
They had passed from doubt to assurance,

from faltering to fidelity, from fear to faith,
from cowardice to courage.
Theirs was no longer a subjective hope,
but a glorious reality.
Their faith was no longer a consoling convenience,
but a consuming compassion.
They were filled with new power;
they proclaimed a new message;
they sang a new song.
Christ had risen from the dead!

What was the change that had taken place
in these disciples?
What was the reason for this fantastic transformation?
It was obviously that
as Christ had risen from the dead,
so they had risen into a new life and experience.
In a strange and incomprehensible sense
they shared in Christ's risen life.
They were soon to discover
in the coming of the promised Comforter,
the Holy Spirit,
that the identical energy which took Christ
out of the grave and raised Him from the dead
was given to them for life,
and vitalized these depressed
and dispirited sons of men
into resurrected personalities and conquering saints.
They were totally convinced
that Jesus was alive again.
The empty tomb, the angels' announcement,
the linen clothes and folded napkin,
the several appearances of Christ Himself—
this was enough for them.
That belief,
along with divinely imparted energy and power,
was sufficient to turn these once whipped
and defeated doubters
into men who were more than conquerors.

On the basis of the well-known Easter effects
   on the disciples,
   I have formulated a thesis.
It is this:
   Out of the masses who wend their way churchward
   in this my generation,
      there are comparatively few who really believe
      that Christ has risen from the dead.
While this may not be the general admission
      of the churchgoers today,
   it is often the unconscious proclamation
   and manifestation of their lives.
I need not, however, look critically toward the church
      or its constituents
   in respect to this state of affairs;
   I need only to look into my own heart
   and to my response to the Easter event.
If Christ really lives,
   and if I really believed that Jesus lives,
   how would this affect my life?
What would or should be my response?

If I really believed that Jesus rose from the dead,
   I would fling aside my garments of self-righteousness,
   the camouflage, the window-dressing of my life,
   and fall on my face before the living Christ
      in repentance of sin.
I would cease at once attempting to deceive
      the almighty God,
   to hide sin and disobedience
      from the living and eternally present Christ.
The Christ who lives to give life,
   to reconcile and to redeem,
   also lives to destroy wickedness
   and to stand in judgment over the unrepentant sinner.

If I really believed in the living Christ,
   He would be the most important factor of my life.
He would take over first place
   among all loyalties and allegiances.

All things else in my life—
   values, loves, affections—
   would be but stepping-stones to that One
   who occupies the throne of the heart,
   the living Christ.

If I *really believed* that Jesus lives,
   my life would be filled with joy unspeakable,
   peace incomprehensible.
I would not be overly anxious about the morrow.
The joy that comes out of my relationship to Him
   would be far greater and more satisfying
   than all the foolish, short-lived thrills
   ˎthis world has to offer.
It would be a peace and assurance that would
      in some measure
   be a witness to the world,
   that might even fill others about me
      with envy and longing
   and draw them to its same Source,
      the living Christ.

If I *really believed* in the resurrected Christ,
   no problem or difficulty, weakness or sin,
   no insufficiency or inadequacy could destroy me.
I would know and experience
   in that power which raised Jesus from the grave
   the grace to overcome my thwarting frailties
   and know that God who did that colossal,
   prodigious act of might and glory
   would not find my problems too difficult,
   that there is available to me
   the same resurrection power
   that brought Christ to life again,
   that the only thing that could possibly limit
   God's resurrection power in my life
   is my stubborn unwillingness
   to commit my faults and failures,
   along with my life,
   to Him.

If I really believed in the risen Christ,
  I would be eager to bypass
    life's conflicts and conveniences,
  even a few legitimate needs,
  and through my living and giving communicate
    the resurrection message
  to others throughout my world.
I would willingly take up the cross assigned to me
  and even through sacrifice and suffering
  seek to extend the kingdom of my loving God,
  made known and made available
  through the crucified and risen Christ,
  to sick and sin-ridden souls around me.

If I really believed that Christ arose from the grave,
  I would cease fretting
  about the godlessness of my world,
  the tumult and turmoil about me.
I would cease worrying about my status and welfare
    on this planet
  and dedicate my energies to the task of proclaiming
  that Christ has risen and is the living Lord.

If I really believed . . .

"If Christ has not been raised," writes a professor,
  "then His mission is uncertificated,
  His miracles are impositions,
  His death is a mistake,
  and Christianity is robbed of its credentials. . . ."
Christ *has* been raised from the dead,
  and because He lives, I too can live—
  in victory over sin
  and as a righteous and holy son of the living God
  now and for all eternity.
If I really believe it.

Whatever might be considered as evidences
  of the resurrection of Jesus,
  the most effective is the witness of God's Spirit
  in the hearts of all who will believe,

the reflection of the living Christ
in the lives of those who follow and obey Him.
It is the kind of evidence
that cannot be denied or disputed.
It can, however, be experienced in my life—
as it has been by unnumbered thousands before me.
God grant that I may confound the skeptics,
in home, office, on Main Street, or in the marketplace,
by a daily demonstration of Christ's resurrection
and by allowing the Christ who arose from the dead
to rise up anew within me and make known
His life and power through me.

When I Really Believe

John 20:19-31

In the early days of this country a very tired traveler
   arrived at the banks of the Mississippi River.
It was early winter,
   and the surface of this great stream
      was covered with ice.
Would he dare to cross over?
   Would the ice bear his weight?
The sky was getting dark,
   and it was necessary that he reach the other side.
After much hesitation he finally got down
      on his hands and knees
   and began very cautiously and fearfully
   to creep across the surface of the ice—
   thinking that by thus distributing
      the weight of his body
   the ice would be less apt to break under him.
When he was about halfway across,
   he heard the sound of singing behind him.
Out of the dusk there came a team-driver
   guiding a four-horse load of coal across the ice
   and singing merrily as he went his carefree way.
Here was the traveler, on his hands and knees,
   trembling lest the ice be not strong enough
      to hold him up.
There, as if whisked along by the winter's wind,
   went the driver, his horses, sleigh, and load of coal
   over the ice on which the traveler
   was so cautiously creeping.

The incident illustrates people's attitude
   toward existence in general.
Whereas some characters barge about the world
   as if it belonged to them,
   others face it timorously and uncertainly,
   treading on tiptoe through its shadowy corridors.

It illustrates, as well, the attitudes of people
    in their relationship to God.
There are, on the other hand,
    those who get down on all fours
    and virtually creep through the Christian experience.
They are the tremulous Thomases of the faith
    and apparently make little, if any, progress in it.
On the other hand, there are
    the passionate Peters and Pauls of Christendom
    who take the Christian walk
    in haphazard leaps and bounds.

I have some envy for Peter and Paul
    and those other apostles of the first-century church
    who saw the risen Christ,
    talked to Him, and were challenged by Him.
Had I been in their sandals,
    I too might be faithful and courageous—
    even to the point of martyrdom.
But I live in a fractured world.
I see so many unsaintly and unsanctified things
        within me and about me
    that bear no resemblance whatsoever
    to the resurrected Christ.
There are problems I cannot solve,
    tragedies I cannot explain,
    conflicts I cannot handle;
    and I become, at times, a tremulous Thomas
    who pines for more tangible evidence
        of divine power—
    that power which was supposed
    to have been made available
    through the resurrection of Jesus
        and the indwelling Christ.

I know what the resurrection of Christ
    has meant to many—
    and what it ought to mean to me.
It promises a happy ending to sin's guilt and control,
    to anxieties and fears,

to inferiorities and inadequacies,
even to the fear of death itself.
It makes possible a new beginning in the life of joy
and effectiveness and love and service.
There are those who fling natural reasoning to the winds
and plunge headlong into the joyous sea
of God's eternal treasures.
There are others who are still standing at the brink
longing for the courage to enter in or,
like the traveler cautiously inching his way
across that river's ice,
are wary and reluctant
about throwing their whole weight
upon Easter's gifts and promises.
I am all too often one of the latter group and,
like the Thomas of the Gospel lesson,
am prone to seek some tangible evidence
of Christ's resurrection power
before I entrust myself
to God's promises and purposes.

I note how kindly Jesus dealt with the skeptical Thomas.
Even the testimony of ten faithful brethren
had no apparent effect on Thomas,
and he doggedly declared:
"Unless I see in His hands the print of the nails . . .
and place my hand in His side, I will not believe."
Yet Jesus did not reject or dismiss him,
but like a gentle nurse dealing with a froward child,
appeared to him and lovingly challenged him.
"Put your finger here, and see My hands;
and put out your hand, and place it in My side. . . ."
If nothing but the coarsest, most physical evidence
could satisfy him, even that was supplied.
Surely this is love which goes beyond human knowledge
and patience and understanding.
Jesus' kindness, however,
was followed by a loving rebuke.
After Thomas joyfully acknowledged

the risen Christ before him,
Jesus said: "Have you believed
    because you have seen Me?
Blessed are those who have not seen
    and yet believe."
While this lack of faith demonstrated by Thomas
    is understandable,
    it is not acceptable.
Unbelief, the parent of every other iniquity,
    not only begets but fosters sin.
Jesus rebukes it wherever He finds it—
    in the case of Peter, whose walking-on-water episode
    ended when the howling winds frightened him
    and he began to sink beneath the waves,
    or when the disciples failed to cast out a demon
        from a little boy
    or when they panicked while sailing
        in a boat in which Jesus was sleeping.
It was unbelief that prevented Moses and Aaron
    from entering the Promised Land
    and turned back the children of Israel
    for another forty-year trek in the wilderness.
Jesus brought Thomas out of his grievious skepticism
    and then pointed him to something better,
    a way of peace and joy and certainty:
    "Blessed are those who have not seen
    and yet believe."

While it was joyous delight for Thomas to know
    by sight and touch that his Lord and God lives,
    Jesus presents him with the key to greater joys,
    the key to true faith,
    the assurance of things not seen.
Christianity does not refuse
    to appeal to human intellect
    or require of its constituents
    a blind, unreasoning faith.
It does, however, ask that they begin
    by believing many things that are above reason

and promises that, so beginning,
    they shall have more light
    and see things more clearly.
As with Thomas, the cry of the skeptic is,
    "If I could, see I would believe."
    The answer of Christ is always,
    "If you would believe, you would soon see . . .
    Blessed are those who have not seen and yet believe."

I have little problem,
    living as I did on a pine-crested mountain,
    in believing in a God of glory and majesty.
This alone, however, does not resolve in a saving faith.
It is necessary that I see Him revealed as a loving,
    forgiving, caring God who knows me by name
    and accepts me as His beloved child.
It is this kind of God that has been revealed to me
    in the life, death, and resurrection of Jesus Christ.
No one could have written as did
    those New Testament writers
    unless they had really known the Christ
    and had witnessed these episodes around His life.
Along with the New Testament proclamations
    of God's loving and saving grace
    is offered the faith to embrace
    that saving love and loving grace.
It begins when I really believe—
    when I stop talking *about* God
    and walk right into His invisible presence
        to talk *to* Him,
    throwing my full weight upon Him,
    plunging into the ocean of His forgiving
    and sustaining grace and love.
I may not feel anything very significant,
    or see miracles take place before my eyes,
    but there will eventually come,
    in response to my believing and obeying,
    a sense of added strength,
    new insight, increased courage,

and the dawning realization that I am in touch
    with divine power,
the same power that raised Jesus from the dead,
the kind that will make a real difference
    in my life.

Take Me to Your Leader

John 10:11-16

If a vehicle from outer space would land on this planet
    and a little green figure
    with one eye and a pointed head
    would pop out and demand that the earth-people
    take him to their leader,
    I wonder where they would take him.

I can guess what the response of some people might be.
Science is my shepherd
    would be the response of those
    who still dream of technological accomplishments
    that will eventually meet the needs of humanity.
The state or government is my shepherd
    would be the cry of multitudes who
        forcibly or willingly
    follow its dictates in blind obedience
    or who are more concerned
    about material and physical security
    than they are about personal freedom.
Education is my shepherd
    might be the cry of humanists and rationalists
    who believe the answers to life
    can be found in the small minds of people.
Property is my shepherd
    is the answer of the materialists
    who pin their hopes on property and possessions.
Pleasure is my shepherd
    is the obvious response of those
    who assume they can find happiness
    in the "if it feels good do it" approach to life.
Religion is my shepherd
    might be the response of sectarians or cultists
    who recognize and honor the existence and significance

of a Creator-God—and then proceed
to confine Him to their own pet formulas
and worship Him on their own terms.

It is more than likely, however,
that most people wouldn't know
where or to whom they could take
this little green fellow
with one eye and a pointed head.
Milton's alarming phrase applies to this day
as accurately as it did to his:
"The hungry sheep look up, and are not fed."
People are looking for shepherds as never before.
The threat of inevitable darkness,
our perilous perch on the precipice of nuclear war,
the feeling of utter helplessness
in the present maze of events,
have resulted in a desperate groping
for something solid and certain to cling to.
Men and women do not know where to go, what to do;
they need someone to follow.

Creating a din of their own,
and adding to the bewilderment of the masses today,
are the cries of dictators and political systems
and campaigning politicians,
of sects and religious movements and organizations
claiming to be able guides
through the present turmoil,
the answer to people's needs,
shepherds destined to lead the sheep.

From the very beginning of His public ministry,
Christ unhesitatingly declared Himself to be
the answer to humanity's needs,
the solution to humankind's quest.
"I am the bread and water of life," He claimed.
"I am the way and the truth and the life . . .
the light of the world . . . the door of the sheep . . .
no one comes to the Father but by Me."

In this Gospel lesson He makes another
of His fantastic claims:
"I am the good shepherd."
Either this Christ is a rabid lunatic—
as are scores of self-appointed "Christs"
enticing the masses today—
or He is truly the Son of God,
for it is this He claims to be.
Moreover, His claims are stronger and more persuasive
than when He first made them,
for He now presents Himself
as the resurrected, living Christ.
He shares no quarters with competitive shepherds,
nor does He get in line
with other religious leaders.
He suggests no scheme for coexistence
with other religious faiths.
He who died for the sins of humankind,
and who conquered over death,
now plants Himself at the helm of humanity
and brazenly announces that He is
the true Shepherd of the sheep.

Jesus gives His reasons
for declaring Himself the good shepherd.
First, He is *owner* of the flock.
"I am the good shepherd;
I know My own and My own know Me."
He is not hired to care for them; He is their owner;
they are His possession.
He knows every one of them
from the time of their birth,
their trials and troubles,
failures and success,
joys and sorrows.
They, the flock of God, constitute His wealth,
for "the Lord's portion is His people."
He values His flock more than anything else.
Only this could have persuaded Him to descend

from heaven's splendor into humanity's bungling,
that of all that shall come to the Father,
He "should lose nothing."
He came to possess His possessions,
  to redeem His sheep,
  to complete and secure His fold.

He is owner; He is also *caretaker* of His flock.
"Behold, He who keeps Israel
  will neither slumber nor sleep,"
  said the psalmist in his understanding of his God.
He is never off-duty,
  but with watchful eye and cocked ear
  is ever attentive to the needs of His lambs.
There are ailing sheep within the flock—
  those who need special attention and care.
He seeks them out and draws them closer to Himself
  and is ready at all times to succor and sustain them.

He is *provider* for the flock.
"He makes me lie down in green pastures;
  He leads me beside still waters. . . ."
In the face of drought or dread enemies,
  a good shepherd is responsible for finding safe,
  fresh pasture land and pure drinking water
    for his sheep.
In like manner Jesus, the true Shepherd,
  supplies the needs of His children
  out of His everlasting riches.
"Seek first His kingdom . . .
  and all these things shall be yours as well,"
  He promised His disciples.
He is the great storehouse
  from which His children derive
  all that is necessary for their well-being.
Truly, "The Lord is my Shepherd; I shall not want."

He is the *defender* of the flock.
The old-time shepherd had all sorts of wild beasts
    to deal with,

but before any enemy could touch his sheep,
    it had to contend with the shepherd.
"They shall never perish, and no one shall snatch them
    out of My hand," promised Jesus
        concerning those who follow Him.

The most important qualification of all
        for true shepherding,
    that which Jesus prophesied in this Gospel lesson
        and which was soon to come to pass
    is that *He lays down His life* for His sheep.
His descent from His Father's right hand,
    His birth in a stable,
    His walk through sorrow's vale among rebellious men,
    His suffering and abuse and persecution,
    and all of this culminating
        in His execution on Calvary's hill,
    were indeed a laying down of His life—
    not for Himself—
    but for all of God's human creatures
        on this earth.

"The Lord is my Shepherd"—and I am *His.*
His child, His disciple, His servant—
    with all the drastic claims,
    the joyous release,
    the reproach and stigma—
    may it be stamped indelibly and eternally
    upon every fiber of my being.
His—may it be my waking thought each morning,
    my heartfelt conviction at every setting of the sun.
I am His property and possession—
    with no rights of my own save the right to sign over
    every right in my life to Him.
This day and every day belongs absolutely
    and unconditionally to Him.
I am His, and not only does His brand
    have its burning imprint upon my life
    but upon everything I touch—my home, my loved ones,
    my associations, my possessions, my work.

They are not mine; they are His.
I am the Master's steward assigned to direct all these
    into usefulness for Him, for they are His.
His—to give Him my burdens, my troubles, my problems—
    and to take in their place His yoke and purpose.
He may send me to some far corner of the world;
    He may allow me sickness, pain, or sorrow;
    He may even make me to be seemingly useless to Him.
Has He done this?
Then I need ask no questions.
Never need I doubt
    His movings and maneuverings in my life.
I am His, for "The Lord is my shepherd."

Life's "Little Whiles"

John 16:16-23

"A little while, and you will see Me no more. . . ."
One doesn't have to live long on this earth
   to discover that the joys and blessings of life
   are interspersed with "little whiles"
   of darkness and despondency.
No one has as yet come up with a way to rid this life
   of its haunting shadows, its hours of pain,
   its overcoming pressures and conflicts.
Oscar Wilde once declared that there was enough suffering
   in a single London lane to deny the existence of God.
There is no place to hide, so many people find ways
   of anesthetizing themselves to life's atrocities,
   attempting to block out the implications
     for their personal lives
   and refusing to involve themselves
   in the agonizing misfortunes of others.
Sooner or later, however, the lights go out.
An earthquake shatters one's security:
   Sickness or loss of job or the death of a loved one
   breaks the bubbles of this earth's creatures
   and they *are* involved—
   in pain, loneliness, darkness,
   in some "little while" of misery
   that pulls down the shrouds about them.

"A little while, and you will see Me no more . . ."
   said Jesus to His disciples.
"What does He mean by 'a little while'?"
   asked the disciples among themselves.
They were soon to find out.
Jesus, their bright star, their supreme hope,
   their love and their joy,
   was brutally torn from them
     and put to death.

It was an overwhelming disaster to the disciples.
It is doubtful that any difficulty or sorrow
    that has come our way,
    can ever surpass the darkness and dismay
    of these awful moments experienced by the disciples.
Then, just a few hours later,
    the sky was ablaze with light.
Their grief-stricken hearts
    were possessed with a new joy.
Sorrow had been transformed into vibrant gladness.
Christ had risen from the dead.
Their "little while" of darkness burst into the dawn
    of a new and glorious day.

"Truly, truly, I say to you, you will weep and lament,
    but your world will rejoice; you will be sorrowful,
    but your sorrow will turn into joy."
It is this same resurrected Christ who stands by today,
    not to shield His followers from suffering and pain,
    problem and conflict, but to ultimately turn
        their "little whiles" of darkness
    into shiny hours of joy and delight.
He stands by as that One who knows full well
    the meaning of these "little whiles" of darkness.
There is no darkness as stifling
    as that which He experienced when He sweat blood
    in the Garden of Gethsemane and prayed:
    "Father, if it be possible,
    let this cup pass from Me . . ."
    or when, in agony on the cross, He cried out:
    "My God, My God, why hast Thou forsaken Me?"
While scores of men and women never proceed
    beyond that excruciating question mark,
    Jesus drank the bitter cup, finished His course,
    and rose victorious over death and suffering.
It is this One,
    who out of the unfathomable dregs of agony
    brought forth eternal joy,
    who even now offers to fill

my "little whiles" of despair
with eternal peace and joy.

My problem today is this:
   how can I latch on to that resurrection power,
   to the living Christ, in such a way as to anchor
   my soul and find inner stability and contentment,
   meaning and purpose, even in the midst
   of my "little whiles" of darkness?
I must *realize* that God
   does not create these "little whiles"
   of suffering and darkness that come my way.
They are, for most part,
   perpetuated by people upon people,
   or are the consequences of God's creatures straying
   from His orbit for their lives, or are created
   by my own carelessness and lovelessness.
      and selfishness.
This by no means explains all suffering,
   but is the basis for much of what afflicts
   this world and its inhabitants.
I must realize that the Christian faith
   does not promise or offer
   complete and immediate deliverance
   from my every pain and conflict—
   that even those who do return and relate to God
   often endure great suffering.
Those who have attempted to make religion
      the immediate and total
   answer to and deliverance from this world's anguish
   have created false religions
   that only camouflage the issues
   and anesthetize people to its reality.
While God cannot be held responsible
      for the troubles that come my way—
   and the spiritual forces of evil
      will attempt to use them to destroy me
      or intercept God's will for my life—
   Easter emphatically declares that these "little whiles"

of darkness and trial can be divinely utilized
to accomplish God's purposes in and through my life.
As the crucifixion of Jesus
was turned into universal blessing,
so the tribulations of God's children
can become blessing and benefit.
God may lovingly permit suffering and pain
to break the sinner's stubborn will
and to make him or her uncomfortable
and unhappy in such rebelliousness,
thereby leading him or her to the eternal joy
of self-surrender and a God-inculcated,
inspired faith.
Or the problems and pains which afflict me
may serve to keep me, who am prone to wander,
close to my Creator,
to purge and polish, purify and prepare me
for higher purposes.

Then, having realized the sin-suffering-death consequence
as estrangement from God,
I must *recognize* that Christ rose from the dead.
Before the sun set on the day of Christ's resurrection,
there was in and about Jerusalem
a company of men and women
who were convinced that Jesus
had risen from the dead.
Sorrow turned into joy, fears into gladness,
doubts into happy assurance.
Their "little while" of dismay and grief was dissolved
because they now recognized the Christ
as their Lord and Savior.
Thus the grace to dissolve or endure my "little whiles"
of depression and darkness
will come with the recognition
of the Risen Christ.
"Have you believed because you have seen me?"
said Jesus to Thomas.
"Blessed are those who have not seen and yet believe."

This is authentic Christianity—to encounter Christ
   and to live in the satisfying consciousness
   that He knows me, my every need,
     my sorrows, my weaknesses;
   that He is always by my side;
   that I am never alone.
He has fathomed the depths of human suffering,
   and He can make my "little whiles" of despair
   less threatening in the light of His joy and life.
He can work out His purpose
   through my hours of suffering
   and teach me how to rejoice
   in the midst of these dark nights
   and through them bring His eternal joy
   to the lives of others.

Having realized and recognized Christ
   in the midst of my "little whiles"
     of darkness and dismay,
   I must *relinquish* my rebellious will,
     my stubborn heart,
   and through Jesus Christ,
   return to God's order and will for my life.
"I want to be me. . . ; I want to be free,"
   cries the songwriter.
I can be both "me" and "free" in the midst of these
   "little whiles" of loneliness and despair.
I must, however, allow Christ to cut me free
    from self-enslavement,
   deliver me from sin and death,
   and grant me life everlasting.
He has done this in the great resurrection event.
It becomes applicable to me the moment I relinquish
   my clutch upon myself and yield to God's reign
   in my life and living.
"So you have sorrow now," said Jesus,
   "but I will see you again
    and your hearts will rejoice. . . .
   Your sorrow will turn into joy . . .

and no one will take your joy from you."
This is the promise, the guarantee,
　　backed by Jesus Christ, who brought life out of death
　　and victory out of defeat by way of the empty tomb
　　and who has performed this very miracle in my life.
"It is the Lord who goes before you,"
　　proclaimed Moses to the Israelites;
　　"He will be with you,
　　He will not fail you or forsake you;
　　do not fear or be dismayed."

The Power Within Us

John 16:5-15

One hears a great deal about power today—electric power,
  horsepower, jet power, atomic power, water power.
People's lives are being guided or sustained
  by some outside source of energy;
  there could be no existence apart from it.
Something people are not too well acquainted with
  or are unconscious about
  is the power within them.
Preachers and therapists speak much about
  the power of positive thinking.
The conditions of the world bear witness to
  the power of negative living.
Much of humanity's suffering has been caused, .
  intentionally or otherwise,
  by the power of human beings to hurt and destroy.
"Death and life are in the power of the tongue,"
  recites a Scriptural proverb.

There is, however, another power within persons,
  or available to them—
  the power to love, create, heal,
  to receive and to reflect joy and peace and goodness.
Though the word itself is not used,
  it is this about which the Gospel lesson speaks.
It is by this power that answers can be found today.
The one antidote for the poison that permeates
  a hate-ridden, hell-bent world
  is the love of God manifested in Jesus Christ.
It was revealed in the person of Christ
  as He walked this earth.
In the midst of sin-ridden humanity
  and earth's ugly atrocities
  He demonstrated a supernatural, divine love—

by healing the sick, giving sight to the blind,
forgiving the sinner,
and comforting the poor and oppressed.
He fought the hate of people with love;
He overcame evil with goodness;
He brought beauty out of ugliness.
At the end of His earthly sojourn, when it appeared
that sin and death had won the battle
and cruel hands nailed Him on the cross,
He arose from the dead,
victorious over sin and death and hell itself,
and demonstrated that heaven's power
was superior to the evil
that has infiltrated this world
and afflicted its inhabitants.

It was Christ's sole purpose to set free divine power
among earth's weaknesses and distortions.
As long as He was here in person and in the flesh, however,
that power was confined to Him
and manifested in the miracles He performed
and the words He spoke.
Thus it was necessary
that He set His face toward Jerusalem,
where the primary purpose of His mission
would be fulfilled.
"It is to your advantage that I go away,"
He said to His disciples.
"If I do not go away,
the Counselor [the Holy Spirit of God],
will not come to you;
but if I go, I will send Him to you."
The disciples understood nothing of this at the time.
They learned later through actual experience
what Jesus was now prophesying.
While Jesus was with them, the divine, supernatural power
so necessary to the salvation of mankind
was confined, constrained, imprisoned,
within the visible Christ.

100

After He performed His mission on this planet
   and returned to His heavenly Father,
   this same divine, supernatural power,
   the same power responsible for Christ's resurrection,
   would return to inhabit and empower
      every one of His disciples.

The visible Christ removed Himself from this world,
   but He did this in order that He might return again
   in all His divine power—clothed in the bodies
   of redeemed sinners (fishermen, tax collectors,
   merchants and farmers, men and women of all races)—
   to continue to bring God's power and persuasion,
   His love and grace, into contact with the sins,
   weaknesses, distortions of humanity.
Everything previous to this had been preparing for it.
The same divine Spirit
   that ministered in the creation of the world,
   producing cosmos out of chaos,
   that had ministered through the visible Christ,
   has now returned to indwell and pour Himself out
   through the lives of every man and woman who would
   in faith and obedience lend themselves
   to His infilling and outflowing.
It means, and I regard this with awe and wonder,
   that everyone who truly embraces this Jesus Christ
   as his or her Lord and Savior, Master and Redeemer,
   becomes the vessel and vehicle
   of His indwelling Spirit and power.
The Christian has within him or her,
   continually at his or her disposal,
   a power far greater than all the natural powers
   within the universe and far superior to the negative
   power and potential for evil and destruction
   that is also harbored in all human flesh.
It is the power to love,
   and out of this the power to create,
   to heal, to bring light into darkness,
   beauty into ugliness, goodness into evil,

sweetness into bitterness,
and joy into grief-stricken situations.
The world of people is distorted, frightened, hungry,
plagued by violence and hatred, sin and guilt.
The loving God knows His ailing and lost sheep
and has the desire and the capability
of healing their wounds and bringing joy and purpose
into their lives.
He has elected to do this,
even limiting Himself in His ability to do this,
through the minds and bodies of men and women
who have been covered by His grace
and bathed in His love.
He has put His Spirit into their hearts and made them
His special and divinely endowed representatives,
assigned to bring His power and provision
into the fractured lives
of the ailing and lost about them.

The Gospel lesson outlines what God's invisible Spirit
proposes to do through His ministers and servants
within this world.
One of His purposes is
to show the world what is wrong with it.
"And when He comes," said Jesus,
"He will convince the world
concerning sin and righteousness and judgment."
Through word and witness, life and example,
Christians are responsible
for allowing God's Spirit through them
to convince and convict this world's inhabitants
concerning the nature of their estrangement
from their Creator.

Another of the Spirit's purposes is to convince humankind
concerning righteousness, *to demonstrate to the world
what is true and right and good and beautiful,*
and to point men and women to meaning and purpose
for their lives.
There is no human righteousness sufficient

to cover humanity's distortions,
but God through Christ offers His own righteousness,
which is more than sufficient
to cover, expiate, and atone for any and every sin
that comes between a person
and the all-righteous and ever-loving God.
Obviously, I cannot get this truth to humanity about me
by verbal proclamation alone.
I am expected to "convince" my world,
people in my arena of responsibility,
not only from the pulpit,
but from workbench, street corner, marketplace,
relating to people wherever they may be found.
I am appointed and empowered to bring Christ to people
by being His Spirit-infilled servant,
identifying with people where they are
and ministering to them at the point of their conscious
as well as their unconscious needs.

Above all, the Holy Spirit,
the power within me and my brothers and sisters
within the Christian faith,
is destined to touch others as God has touched us.
As God reaches me in my need,
so I have been empowered to bring Him to others
in their need—through love.
There is no other way.
As Christ descended into my sin-ridden life
to lovingly identify Himself with my sin
and bear its eternal consequences,
so I, empowered by His Spirit,
am appointed to identify myself
with the sins, weaknesses, sufferings, and needs
of my fellow persons
and share in the burden of bearing them.
When I give myself to others in love,
the divine love of God can reach through—
to purify and sanctify my love
and touch the needs of people with the divine love

103

which resolves in forgiveness, healing, strength,
    joy, and purpose.

It is time that I cease being a clod
    that clutters up the church of Christ
    and become what I am destined to be—
    a vibrant, pulsating vehicle of spiritual power.
That power is within me.
I need only to submit to the source,
    the invisible Christ,
    and yield myself totally
    to His control and use.

Teach Me to Pray

John 16:23-30

I have considered the consequences of Easter—
    what it was designed to mean and ought to mean
      in my life.
I accept my Lord's enablement,
    the gift of His Spirit,
    and His commission
    to continue the incarnation of Christ
    among this world's citizens.
I am commanded to "go,"
    to represent and reflect Him
    to people about me.
I am not, however, thrust out unarmed, unequipped,
    and alone in this chaotic world.
He is with me always, invisibly undergirding,
    inspiring, empowering, and guiding
He meets my personal needs—
    and He can transmit through me
    what is necessary to help meet the needs
    of others in my path.

Something that is very important for me
    to recognize and utilize
    is the means given me to enable me to communicate
    between this tangible, three-dimensional world
      in which I live
    and that invisible, many-dimensional universe
      that is ruled by God.
I, along with all of Christ's disciples,
    am the child and servant of God,
    redeemed and consecrated
    to carry out His purposes on this planet.
While God's children ultimately belong
    to the infinite and eternal dimensions of God,
    this is not visible to human creatures

and they must use a sort of sixth sense
which bridges the gap
between the visible and temporal world
and the invisible, eternal universe of God.
This sixth sense might be called faith.
One of its instruments or faculties is called prayer.

Prayer, as I presently understand it,
    is not confined to the "Thees" and "Thous"
    of some archaic prayer book.
It is not restricted to bowed heads and folded hands—
    to a church altar
    or even to a particular time each day.
It is not more authentic
    if one kneels or falls on one's face
    to grovel in penitence.
It doesn't have to be written or carefully memorized.
Prayer is, in essence, a free-flowing,
    ongoing relationship of faith with a loving God.
It can be reflected in numerous ways—
    in fine literary phrases or great choral renditions,
    in unspoken feelings,
    in groans of agony or explosions of adoration,
    in singing or crying or laughter or tears.
Some people address themselves to prayer
    at a particular time each morning;
    others walk in prayer
    throughout every hour of the day.
Some people express their needs to God
    or their adoration for God
    in well-chosen phrases;
    others feel great concern or need or gratitude
    and perpetually commit it to God
    in their unspoken feelings and faith.
Prayer is really a state of grace,
    a constant, continual openness to God,
    a trust and confidence in Him
    as He is revealed through Jesus Christ,
    a daily walking with God.

In this Gospel lesson Jesus was teaching His disciples
the rudiments of this kind of communication with God.
"Truly, truly, I say to you, if you ask anything
of the Father, He will give it to you in My name. . . .
Ask, and you will receive, that your joy may be full."
On another occasion He said to them:
"Ask, and it will be given you;
seek, and you will find;
knock, and it will be opened to you."
This is, no doubt, the level of prayer life
that all Christians begin with
and return to from time to time.
It may be understood as the level or plateau
of childlike prayer.
It is usually verbal and is most often focused
upon specific requests or pleas
for God's action on behalf of His children
or for God's gifts in view of certain needs.
This may not be prayer in its most profound sense,
but if entered into sincerely, it is prayer,
and Christians never get so wise or sophisticated
that they don't need this kind of prayer at times
in their lives.
"Give us this day our daily bread," prayed Jesus
in what is called the Lord's Prayer.
Nevertheless, this can become selfish prayer,
God-manipulating prayer
prayer that seeks to use God to further personal ends
rather than seeking to accomplish His purposes.

There is another level of prayer life
that tends to be more rigid, disciplined,
sometimes liturgical and formalistic—
or it may be a more aggressive pursuit
of what one assumes to be God's will for him or her
and a persistent pressure upon God
to make it come to pass.
This kind of praying also has its place
in the lives of most Christians.

The author of the Letter to the Hebrews
    enjoins his readers
  to "leave the elementary doctrine of Christ
    and go on to maturity,"
  suggesting the need to turn from milk to solid food
  in respect to growing up in the faith.
This also may be valid in respect to prayer life
  and suggests a higher plateau
  in one's communication with God.
There may be less rigidity.
The old forms of discipline, once so important,
  are less binding.
There is less dependence on words and more concern
  for an ongoing relationship with a loving God
Christians at this stage are not so likely to be mastered
  by the winds of circumstance.
Security is no longer their primary concern.
They need not run screaming to God
  when their landmarks change
  or cling desperately to Him
  if the sands shift beneath them.
They know that they belong to God and they don't have
  to hold on to Him, because He holds on to them.
They are God's children, and they need not badger Him
  for their daily needs any more than little children
  need to beg their earthly parents
  for their daily necessities.
They will still rely on words at times,
  verbalizing their feelings
  of depression or shame or exaltation.
They may fall on their faces in confession—
  or rise up to dance in praise and celebration.
Prayer for them, however, is a more perpetual thing,
  a walking with God, abiding in Him,
  a relationship with Him.

Some of my prayers are childish.
There are other times when I rush about
  on the adolescent level,

seeking some sign of God's favor or guidance.
Now and then I believe I do make some progress
    toward the more mature level of a God-son relationship
    and feel strongly that this is the higher,
    more profound plateau that I must aspire to
    and expect, by God's grace, to reach.
Just what is mature or high-level prayer?
Prayer is *faith*—taking God at His Word
    irrespective of one's innermost feelings about it.
The ecstasy that was so important
    in the adolescent stage of Christian growth
    is not so important anymore.
One will rejoice in such feelings when they come
    without insisting upon their presence
    as proof of God's love and grace.
The mature Christian knows
    that he or she is God's beloved child
    and that He will provide His children what they need
    in His own good time.

Prayer is *obedience*—a commitment of one's life
    to God and His purposes and principles
    as revealed through Jesus Christ
    regardless of the cost or consequence
    to property, possessions, or life.
Indeed, this level of prayer
    will never be the experience
    of those who are not willing
    to pay that kind of price
    or those who are not willing
    to "deny themselves and take up their cross"
    to follow Jesus Christ.
Nor will they ever know the deep joy,
    the inner security and serenity—
    even in the midst of the tempest and tumult—
    that accompanies this kind of a relationship to God.

Prayer is *concern*—
    not primarily for oneself, but for others.
This will take the form of verbal intercession,

110

and certainly unuttered and unexpressed petitions,
on behalf of one's neighbor who is in need;
but it must, as well, take the form of loving,
sacrificial service to God's needy children
wherever they can be reached and served.

Whatever the level or plateau of my relationship to God,
it is essential that I communicate with Him—
relate, trust, obey Him—and this remains possible
only when I submit my life and surrender myself to Him
as He is revealed through Jesus Christ.
It means, as well, that I listen to Him
as He speaks to me through Word and the Sacrament,
and through the agonies and needs,
the joys and experiences of my fellow persons.
Above all, I am assured that God loves me;
no matter how great my failures or fallibilities,
He loves me and is here with me
and is waiting for me to entrust my life to Him
and to enlist in His eternal purposes.

The Spirit of the Lord Is Upon Me

John 14:23-31

A renowned preacher once made the observation
    that "what passes among us in these days for Christianity
      is very thin stuff,"
    that modern religion is altogether
      too "cozy, comfortable, and conventional."
Many of those who built new churches
    and enlarged church rolls following WWII
    equated Christianity with middle-class Americanism—
    snubbing original Christians
      as too extreme
    and toning down Christ's initial challenge
      as too radical—
    and were possibly inoculated
      with a mild form of religion
    that served to make them immune
      to the real thing.
While many things have improved since then,
    there are still some church members
    who hold views about God which are orthodox enough
    according to New Testament doctrines
    and yet have no real knowledge of them.
They have some understanding of the revelation of God
    and the reconciliation with God
      that comes through Christ
    without its being experienced in their lives.
They respect the creeds of the worship service
    without these being the real expression of their hearts.
They read the words of the Bible
    without hearing the Word of God.

God's judgment begins with the house and family of God.
It begins even with me.
Before I criticize the evils of society,
    or accentuate the negative

in terms of what is going on
in the church, nation, or world,
I had better look to my relationship with God.
I need to determine if my faith is real,
or if it is Christianity without Pentecost,
a Christianity devoid of the Holy Spirit.

The Person and the work of the Holy Spirit
is by necessity a mysterious doctrine.
Spiritual, unseen, intangible, infinite,
the power of God through His invisible Spirit
can never be understood by mortals.
It can, however, be experienced.
Jesus made it known to His disciples
that it was necessary for Him to leave them,
for only then could the Spirit of God
take over their lives.
The Holy Spirit, who was up to this time
confined to the Person of Christ,
would hereafter be able to work
when and where and how He chooses
in and through the life of every man and woman
who follows Jesus Christ.
He would in this way make possible the fulfillment
of that strange promise of Jesus when He said:
"He who believes in Me
will also do the works that I do;
and greater works than these will he do,
because I go to the Father."
The Holy Spirit through Jesus Christ
made God living and real to the disciples.
Through the disciples of Jesus,
from that time until this,
the Spirit makes God living and real
to other men and women,
who in turn become the disciples and servants,
sons and daughters of the living God.
Religion becomes much more than a theory,
a fad or fashion, a Sunday-morning habit.

It becomes a vital, paramount, everyday experience
in the life of every person
who yields to His indwelling and control.

In this Gospel lesson, Jesus is declaring
what the Holy Spirit will mean to His beloved disciples
whom He was soon to leave behind.
"He will teach you all things," said Jesus
concerning the promised Counselor, the Holy Spirit,
and thereby points to the coming,
invisible Spirit of God
as the key to success and fulfillment
and the One to follow and rely upon.

Pentecost declares that God is here,
occupying the hearts and lives,
working out His purposes through the bodies and beings
of all men and women who truly and totally
commit themselves to God
as revealed through Jesus Christ.
The Gospel lesson states
some of the things the Holy Spirit
would teach me in this hour—
what He desires to work out in and through me.
For one thing, should the Holy Spirit have His way
within me,
He would teach me *the meaning of love.*
"If a man loves Me," said Jesus, "He will keep My Word,
and My Father will love him, and We will come
to him and make Our home with him. . . ."
The Holy Spirit teaches me that love is the entire
meaning and content of the Christian life.
It is the central and controlling factor
for my understanding of the life
to which God calls me in Christ.
It is true that "we love because He first loved us."
"God so loved the world that He gave His only Son. . . ."
God initiated love; He *is* Love.
But the Holy Spirit teaches that such love

demands a response on the part of humankind
and that there is no relationship to God
apart from such a response.
While I can avidly profess such love for God—
    and should—
the only way I can manifest or demonstrate
such love for God
is by way of loving my fellow beings.

The Holy Spirit, should He have His way in me,
    would teach me *the meaning of obedience.*
"If a man loves Me, he will keep My Word . . ." said Jesus;
    "he who does not love Me does not keep My words."
Inextricably intertwined with love of God
    is obedience to God.
Paul, in writing to the church at Rome, once stated:
    "The law of the Spirit of life in Christ Jesus
    has set me free from the law of sin and death."
This freedom, however,
    is not just freedom *from* something—
    freedom from hang-ups and addictions,
    fears and doubts,
    the many things which plague God's servants—
    it is freedom *for* something.
I am set free to obey God.
Family or friends, economic pressures or social demands,
    even the laws of civil government,
    must not interfere or trifle with
    my freedom to obey God.
"For all who are led by the Spirit of God
    are the sons of God," wrote Paul.
Only those who claim that Spirit,
    follow the Spirit, and walk in obedience
    to the dictates of the Spirit of God,
    can truly be considered to be
    God's sons and daughters.
It is this that determines whether or not
    one's Christianity rises above the pulpit-pounding,
    pew-warming state of religion

into a heart-loving and life-giving
   relationship to God.
It is this that reveals whether or not
   one's Christian experience and witness
   includes Pentecost and is motivated by the Holy Spirit.
It is not whether or not one speaks in strange tongues,
   or has ecstatic, out-of-this-world experiences,
   but whether or not one walks in obedience
   to the words of Jesus Christ.
"If a man loves Me, he will keep My Word. . . ."

The Holy Spirit seeks to teach me *the meaning of peace.*
"Peace I leave with you; My peace I give to you;
   not as the world gives do I give to you.
   Let not your hearts be troubled,
   neither let them be afraid."
This is what multitudes in this world are seeking—
   even through drugs, orgies
      and all sorts of bizarre activities—
   but which can be found and fulfilled
   only by the indwelling and empowering
      of the Holy Spirit.
It is peace in the midst of conflict,
   calm in the midst of storm,
   joy in the midst of sorrow,
   life in scorn of consequences.
It involves danger and risk;
   it promises trouble and persecution;
   it challenges to self-sacrifice and suffering;
   it guarantees real meaning and purpose
      and life everlasting.

The last words of the Gospel lesson flash the signal
   for launching out, taking off—
   the green light for loving, obedient, risk-filled,
   sacrificial service to the world about me.
"Rise," said Jesus, "let us go hence."
"Move out," the Lord of the church would say
   to me today.

117

"You have been set free
   from the shackles of sin and self-concern;
   you have been redeemed and reconciled
   and reshaped for the God-movement.
You are in the movement—now *move.*
You have the power, the equipment—
   My invisible and eternal presence in your life.
Stop dawdling, sitting around crying
   about your personal problems
   or waiting for some kind of ecstatic feeling
   or supernatural sign.
You have everything you need to be My son and servant,
   My vessel and vehicle, communicator and transmitter
   to people in your community and world.
I'll go with you; I'll abide within you;
   I'll work out My purposes through you;
   I will love and keep you forever.
Now go . . . go . . . go. . . ."

How to Start Over Again

John 3:1-15

One of the most precious gifts
   that life can hand out to people
   is the opportunity and privilege
   to begin anew—to start over again.
It happens to most people at one time or another.
Enterprising people may fail in some business venture
   only to start over again with hopes of succeeding.
A marriage relationship falls apart
   but can often, with forgiving love
     and renewed trust in one another,
   find new meaning and purpose.
It is comparable to a sort of second birth,
   a second chance to achieve something,
   to succeed or make good.

This is the thesis of this Gospel lesson.
It underlines the necessity
   and proclaims the possibility
   of a new birth,
   and this on the basis that man and woman's first birth
   is a cataclysmic failure.
It intimates that there is a chaotic rift
   between Creator and creature,
   that a soul-destroying disharmony
   reigns throughout the observable universe.
This planet, in particular,
   appears to be out of orbit with its Creator
   and wandering aimlessly without destiny or purpose
   through the eternal darkness
   of a cold, unfriendly universe.
This disharmony and discordance became an integral part
   of man and woman's nature.
"All have sinned and fall short of the glory of God,"
   wrote St. Paul.

119

"There is none that does good, no, not one,"
   proclaims ancient Scripture.

Inculcated into men and women's souls, however,
   is the longing for better things,
   the grasp for perfection,
   the urge for something which hovers tantalizingly
   beyond their reach.
History, by and large, is the record of humanity's
   desperate but futile attempts
   to do something about society's
      disorder and disharmony
   and to find order and unity and wholesomeness.
People try through reason and logic
   to find their way out of the night.
They formulate laws and statutes
   to bring order to this planet.
They create religions to give humankind
   something beyond itself to focus upon.
Education, the arts, science—
   even force and coercion—
   are used in the attempt
   to bring order out of confusion
   and to convince or compel people
   to live at peace with one another.
While much of this has been of some value,
   the world continues to become increasingly insecure,
   and its brutalities mount in intensity.
People begin to realize
   that the ultimate answer to society's ills
   is not to be found in reformation
      or education or science,
   and multitudes turn wantonly
   to sensuality or materialism in the effort to numb themselves
   to the feeling of utter helplessness.

All is not utter hopelessness, however.
There is a solution.
It is verbalized by Jesus in this Gospel lesson.
It has to do with a second chance, a new beginning,

a new birth, with the opportunity to start over again.
The first step toward a true solution
    of humanity's ills
  is *confrontation*.
It means that people face up to their humanity
    and the problems and conflicts that evolve from it.
Nicodemus did this in a rather disguised manner
    by coming to Jesus at night—
    recognizing that there was a basic emptiness
    in his life despite his wealth and position.
I can't afford to be so subtle.
Maybe some people can hide their distortions
        better than others
    but the fact of disorder and disharmony
        exists in every human heart.
Confrontation is the process of recognizing it,
    facing up to it.
I have tried to justify it or repress it,
    acting as if it did not exist.
If that fails I may even resort to blaming others
    for my wrongdoings and the resultant guilt.
    The first step toward a solution
        of the problem of guilt
    is confrontation,
    the acceptance of my finitude,
    recognition of my guilt,
    and the prayer of the publican in the temple,
    "God, be merciful to me, a sinner!"

Following confrontation, there is *regeneration*.
It concerns the good news of the love and acceptance
    of a forgiving God, and is applicable
    only to those who are guilty
    and who recognize their need of God's grace.
The self-righteous Pharisees
    never experienced God's grace
    because they refused to be confronted
    with their sin and guilt—
    or assumed that it could be obliterated

by their fanatical observance of laws and rituals.
It was people like the publican in the temple,
    the prodigal son, the woman caught in the act,
    the tax collector who pilfered the state's receipts,
    who experienced the peace and joy of divine forgiveness
    because they acknowledged their sin and guilt
    and received God's mercy.
Regeneration is represented by Christ's exhortation
        to Nicodemus:
        "Truly, truly, I say to you,
    unless one is born anew,
    he cannot see the kingdom of God. . . .
    You must be born anew."
Jesus is saying, in effect, that God is already aware
    of the failure and inadequacy of original birth,
    the sinful nature into which His creatures are born,
    and their utter incapability
        of doing anything about it.
Though He cannot tolerate or condone sin in any form,
    being the just and righteous God that He is,
    He made a way whereby He could accept
    His earthborn creatures as they are—
    sinful, weak, failure-fraught—
    and begin to make them
    into what He intended them to be,
    restoring them to His order
    and will for their lives.
He made it possible for His children
    to be *born* all over again.

"You must be born anew."
The exhortation of Jesus throbs
    with urgency and necessity.
How can this be?
Can a man enter a second time into his mother's womb
    and be born?" was Nicodemus' question.
"As Moses lifted up the serpent in the wilderness,"
    responded Jesus, "so must the Son of man be lifted up,
    that whoever believes in Him may have eternal life."

123

Christ's answer to Nicodemus was probably
   without meaning at this time,
   but there is reason to believe
   that the seed sown by Christ's statement
   eventually grew into a beautiful flower
   of understanding and experience
   in the life of that man.
I ought to know well what it means,
   this new birth of faith in Jesus Christ
   and His bearing of my sin and guilt on the cross
      on my behalf.
It is on this basis that He accepts me
   in loving forgiveness and pardon
   and restores me to Himself
      and His purposes for my life.

It is not directly addressed,
    but certainly intimated in this Gospel lesson,
    that regeneration resolves
       into *transformation*.
"Do not be conformed to this world," wrote Paul,
   but be transformed by the renewal of your mind,
   that you may prove what is the will of God,
   and what is good and acceptable and perfect."
Regeneration does not mean the end to guilt feelings,
   nor the sin and human weaknesses that cause them.
They are forgiven—past, present, and future—
   but the ability to sin and the inevitability
   of falling and failing remains.
I am still residing in the sin-permeated body
   with which I was born
   even while I bask in my new birth
   within the embrace of God's acceptance and love.
"I do not do the good I want," said the apostle Paul,
   "but the evil I do not want is what I do . . .
   wretched man that I am!"
This is the day-by-day experience of the child of God
   in human flesh, and this will continue to foster
      sin and guilt.

Then Paul breaks forth into a hymn of triumph:
    "Thanks be to God through Jesus Christ our Lord. . . .
    There is therefore now no condemnation
    for those who are in Christ Jesus."
The Christian simultaneously experiences
    the sharp consciousness of guilt
    and the vivid certainty of grace.
They cannot be separated in this life.
Both are necessary to my growth and maturity
    as a Christian.
It is not the sense of sin or sinning that is removed
    by new birth or regeneration,
    but rather the condemnation of it.
I am a sinner; I shall always in this life be a sinner.
In facing up to my sin and guilt I am only drawn
    closer to the eternal love of God through Christ,
    who has removed its condemnation
    and who accepts me as His "born again" child.

The Gospel of Jesus Christ is the glad and glorious news
    that God makes available to every man and woman
    that forgiving grace which enables him or her
    to start over again.
"For freedom Christ has set us free," wrote Paul.
I am free to start over again,
    free to be ever transformed by God's Spirit
    into what He intends for me to be,
    free from the fear of death,
    free to risk reputation, material security,
    even life itself, in the pursuit of divine purposes
    and of love and justice and equality
        for every human creature.

The Two-Sided God

Luke 14:16-24

The parable that makes up this Gospel lesson
   is a remarkable portrayal of a two-sided God,
   One who manifests both a sunny south side
   as well as a stormy north side,
   and One whom every person must eventually face.
Humankind cannot choose whether or not to stand
   before the eternal and almighty God.
This is predestined.
People do choose, however,
   or by their daily choices do determine,
   which side of this God
   they are to know and experience.

The parable in question, first of all,
   presents that which I like to hear about—
   and need to hear about again and again—
   the sunny south side of God.
A great banquet is prepared—representing all things
   a person needs for fulfillment—
   the quenching of thirst, the satiating of hunger,
   the lightening of burdens, and promises to put
   meaning, purpose, joy, and contentment
   into his or her drab or hectic or panic-ridden life.
It is a picture of the perpetual
   willingness and readiness of God
   to receive and reconcile people to Himself
"Come," said the host of this story,
   "for all is now ready."
Never was so much put into so few words.
It refers to God's wonderful feast of good things
   prepared for those creatures
   He formed in His own image.
It reviews for God's creatures
   His unfathomable love and mercy.

126

Man and woman were created to be the apple of His eye,
   His heart's desire, the objects of His devotion.
"Come, for all is now ready."
The menu of this sumptuous feast
   includes all that God's creatures need to make them
      eternally happy:
   the forgiveness of all their sins,
   love and acceptance as God's own sons and daughters,
   meaning and significance as individuals,
   strength and courage to stand up
      against life's perplexing problems,
   wisdom and guidance to illuminate
      the dark paths of human existence,
   purpose and plan for ordered living,
   power and peace in the midst of tragedy and pain,
   hope and promise of life everlasting.
"Come, for all is now ready."
There is nothing a person needs to do except to come—
   to receive.

This is the sunny south side of God—
   inviting, entreating, promising, receiving—
   and it is extended to everyone
   regardless of race or station, age or intelligence,
   past sin, present complications, or future fears.
And this, of course, is the Gospel—
   the good news of another,
   totally different kind of life
   than that which the average person
      acknowledges and pursues.
It comes to God's creatures through His Son.
Jesus not only preached about this love of His Father;
   He became the Gift of love.
He gave humanity this love
   through His death and resurrection.
He initiated a ministry of love and reconciliation
   that He passed on to all
   who thereby became reconciled to God through Him.
The Gospel is good news because it makes its way

into the ugly situations of life and works for change.
It is news that every person
  needs to hear and to act upon
  in his or her particular situation.
It is as relevant in this, the twentieth century,
  as it was in the first.

The Gospel is revolutionary news.
It makes every human creature
  the very son or daughter of God.
It demands the change, the transformation
  of those who hear and embrace it,
  from self-centered egotists
  into sacrificial lovers of all humankind
  and turns His beloved children into agents of change
  that are commissioned to be communicators, enablers,
  facilitators of change throughout the world.

The Gospel is radical news.
It invites the human creature
  to radical decisions and actions.
It points to conversion and surrender
  and self-abandonment.
It spells out a new orbit, a new focus, a new goal,
  new attitudes and motivations.
It transforms people from leeches into lovers,
  from children of darkness into children of light,
  from slaves of self-centered living
  into the very brothers and sisters of Jesus Christ.
It is most certainly news of sin's forgiveness,
  but it is more than that.
It is the news of deliverance from sin's power
  and the freedom to become vigorous, active,
  God-empowered servants and ministers
  sent out to lead others
  to the joy and freedom of God's love.

To those who are guilt-ridden
  the Gospel is the good news of divine pardon.
To those who are isolated and alienated

it is the good news of God's
ever-present care and concern.
To those who are despondent
over the meaninglessness of existence
it is the good news of God's purposes for life
as revealed in His Son, Jesus Christ.
To those who are tired of living and afraid of dying
it is the good news of resurrection and life eternal.
To the depressed and oppressed children of society
it is the good news of God's affirmation and love
of every human creature in every time and place.

"Come, for all is now ready."
This is the sunny south side of God,
His invitation to this great feast of good things,
an invitation extended to the whole of humanity
throughout all the world.
What a feast it is!
Love, peace, joy, meaning and purpose,
validity, and identity, everlasting life.
It is the answer to a person's deepest longings,
the fulfillment of his or her most intense hungers,
the very purpose of a human being's creation
on this planet upon which he or she lives.

There is also, according to this parable,
a stormy north side of God.
"For I tell you, none of those men who were invited
shall taste my banquet."
The host was referring to those invitees
who excused themselves from coming
to the great banquet—
who found reasons for not accepting
the invitation of the Master.
"Many are called, but few are chosen,"
said Jesus at another time in His ministry.
It intimates that the God who is persistently rejected
must ultimately reject the very people He once invited
but who refused to come to His feast of good things.

130

What is so unfortunate is that the people
  who refuse or neglect the invitation of God
  to the great feast of life
  are often hardly aware of what they are doing.
Perhaps they have fabricated a concept of God
  as perpetually sunny—
  a smiling, tolerant, condoning God
  who is accepting of anything they do,
  a permissive grandfather in the sky
  who stands by to solace and save when things go wrong,
  a parachute to resort to when life's motors conk out.
Maybe they accept only as much of God as they can handle,
  or create their own image of God—
  the kind that will respond to their selfish desires.
Then they proceed to possess this God,
  wrap their affections around such a God;
  this becomes obvious in that their faith
  does nothing to make them more loving, caring,
  and concerned about other people around them.
There are others who adopt a style of life
  that apparently numbs them to their basic needs
  a morality, a set of rules, a discipline, a tradition
  that satisfies them for the moment—
  and they feel no need for anything else.
They convince themselves that God is on their side
  and pay their dues by giving Him
  a Sunday-morning corner in their lives.
They may be refusing the invitation to the great banquet
  because their primary focus, their reason for living,
  is centered upon this temporal world and all its wares.
According to the parable,
  some of these may never be included
    in that great banquet.
They are invited, but they refuse to come.

It is late, but there is still time to discover
  the sunny south side of the living God
  and to feast on the eternal delicacies
    of His banquet table.

131

He seeks even in this moment
   to draw this world's citizens,
   His created children, to Himself,
   and then to commission them to go out
   to the highways and byways
   and share with others what they have received
   as sons and daughters of the living, loving God.
"Come, for all is now ready."

"Get the Hell Out"

Luke 16:19-31

When the American Standard Version of the Holy Bible
    appeared about a century ago,
      a man came into an English book shop and asked for
      a copy of that "new Bible without any hell in it."
The attitude expressed thereby has been a characteristic
    of many people throughout the history of Christianity—
    those who are trying to "get the hell out" of
      theology and Christian teaching.
This is not surprising.
Renowned preachers of the past
    painted with lurid adjectives
    the unending torments of the damned
    and even talked and wrote
    of the pleasures of the redeemed
    who were supposedly given ringside seats
    so that they might watch the agony
    of unhappy victims in hell.
The saintly, kindly Thomas Aquinas declared:
    "In order that nothing be wanting to the happiness
    of the blessed in heaven,
    a perfect view is granted them
    of the tortures of the damned."
Jonathan Edwards wrote:
    "The sight of hell's torments will exalt
    the happiness of the saints forever;
    it will give them a more lively relish."
Such ghastly concepts revolt human sensibilities
    and are not justified by the New Testament.
Today, however, the tendency is very much
    toward the other extreme.
One almost never hears a sermon preached
    on the subject of hell,
    and humankind derides it,
    rationalizes it out of existence,

ignores it, disbelieves it,
laughs at it, jokes about it,
and does everything possible
to "get the hell out" of
     the realm of serious contemplation,
obliterating it once for all.

It is not possible to get rid of hell
     by simply wishing it out of existence.
"Drive her out," said Emerson,
     "and she comes running back."
The possibility of its being a fact,
     a reality, a condition, even a place
     continues to be a sharp pinprick
     in the complacency of the multitudes
     who want a freer conscience
     in their endeavors to live unto themselves.
There are enough of hell's symptoms and manifestations
     around them to make them aware that there is basis
     for the doctrine and teaching of hell.
While there is probably no doctrine or teaching
     that we would be more willing
          to remove from Christianity,
     the teaching of hell has the support of Scripture
     and even the words of Jesus Christ.

Of course hell is a repugnant doctrine.
The fact that it does exist, however,
     is obvious to all about us.
God did not create it; He only made heaven
     and all things to have the nature of heaven.
God's children were created for heaven, not for hell.
Hell was brought into existence,
     according to the traditional teaching,
     when Satan and his followers deliberately broke away
     from God's love and established for themselves
     a kingdom of darkness.
Man and woman,
     in their freedom to disobey their Creator-God,
     followed suit—

and ever since there has come to be
a spot of hell in every human creature.
Thus two kingdoms, heaven and hell, light and darkness,
love and hate, good and evil, joy and sorrow,
beauty and ugliness, exist and are in conflict
in the very midst of humanity.
The agonies endured, the sufferings witnessed,
the terrible calamities and catastrophes
that befall human creatures,
the insurmountable problems
that afflict and torment,
the compulsions and obsessions
that drive and distress—
there is some measure of hell in all this.
This may, however, be hell in a very limited sense,
for the love of God is still present and ever active
with healing and hallowing, illuminating,
comforting, redeeming, and empowering.
When one tries to visualize a world
in which God's love and grace were totally removed
from this planet,
and joy and light and truth and beauty
forever extinguished,
he would come as close as he cares to
in respect to the meaning and extent of hell.

Jesus' parable in our Gospel lesson was not intended
to present a literal description of either heaven or hell.
It can, nonetheless, give some insight
into certain principles that appear to apply
to the hell referred to throughout the Scriptures.
The rich man is condemned—not because of his riches
but because he was a materialist
and they took the place of God in his life.
According to this parable, he found that life after death
was a life or existence immersed in *torment*.
His gratification of self in his earthly life—
even to the extent of ignoring the crying needs
of the beggar at his gate—

may have stifled the longing of his soul
    for spiritual blessings.
Now these longings that scream for fulfillment
    are impossible to stifle and have no hope of fruition.

He discovered that life after death included *memory*
    of the past—failures, lost opportunities,
    neglect of God and His purposes,
    rank self-centeredness—
    and they are memories that plague him incessantly.
The parable implies, also,
    that this after-death state of the materialist
    was a *final* state.
The chasm between the rich man
    and the life that Lazarus now enjoyed
    was impassable or unbridgeable.
One may escape the hell endured in this life—
    or at least find heaven's grace to endure it.
There is, in this life, a bridge of salvation
    that leads to God,
    a way of life eternal for every human being.
Those who reject it are choosing hell in its present form,
    choosing to deny spiritual values
    in favor of material abundance or sensual delights.
The consequence, if people continue in their rejection,
    is the experience of that final and irrevocable hell
    from which there is no returning.

The parable indicates that there is *no excuse*
    for this materialist's state in hell.
It was the result of lifetime choices.
Even now there was apparently no indication of sorrow
    or penitence in view of such unfortunate choices—
    only fear and despair under the torment of hell.

Those who would like to "get the hell out" of
    the teachings of Christianity
    probably have little idea
    of the enormous price God has already paid
    to remove the fact of hell

when He through Jesus Christ became man
and died by torture in order to break the hold
of sins and its consequences upon His creatures.
Herein is the problem—and the tragedy:
There is so much mercy, and still there is hell.

It appears that few people today
are really concerned about the threat of hell
beyond this life or dispensation.
It is the hell of the present moment,
the hell about them,
that drives them to despair.
The physical pain, the mental agony,
the uncertainty and insecurity of this hour—
this is for many people a vicious kind of hell.
There are multitudes of people,
many within a stone's throw of most churches,
who are living in hell—
the hell of loneliness, of deprivation, of addiction,
of hate or pain or depression or fear.

The good news of the Gospel is that there is deliverance
from the hell that afflicts people today—
be that hell real or imaginary.
It begins with the acknowledgement of one's finitude,
of sin, failures, mistakes in his or her life,
and the acceptance of God's loving forgiveness.
I find this to be not a once-for-all experience,
but a now-and-always relationship to God.
Having acknowledged with sorrow my personal involvement
in the hellish conditions
that exist within and about me,
I need no longer to brood over past errors
but rather to accept God's acceptance of me as I am
and to commit myself to His reign and control
of my life.
This means I must dedicate myself
to God's purposes as well,
to be Christ-incarnate,
a channel and communicator of God's love and power

into the hell that exists around me.
There is no other way to "get the hell out" of my life—
  and even out of the lives
    of people whose lives I touch—
  and to eliminate forever any fear of hell
  in that glorious life eternal that Jesus guarantees
  through His death and resurrection
  on behalf of all God's creatures.

The Case of the Potted Christian

Luke 5:1-11

There is a method of stunting trees so that they never
  grow higher than a couple of feet.
It is done by tying off the taproot so that the tree
  is forced to live off its surface roots.
These trees beautify unique little gardens
  making them places of supreme beauty,
  but perform little service beyond that.
They are rather useless in terms of supplying lumber
  for building or for shelter against raging typhoons.
They become potted plants instead of the forest giants
  they were originally intended to be.

A baby in a crib is a beautiful sight to behold,
  but if that creature, plagued by some crippling disease,
  remains a crib-baby after twelve or fifteen years,
  it becomes a tragic and pitiful sight indeed.
Even more tragic, though of far less concern to people,
  are the moral and spiritual dwarfs
  who have never attained to the height and stature
    they are destined for
  and who are potted plants instead of forest giants
  because their taproots are tied off
  and they have never gone deep
  into an intimate relationship with God
  to draw on divine sustenance and strength.
It is apparent, this shallowness,
  in almost every facet of their lives—
  moral, cultural, social, spiritual.
It is portrayed in their attitudes and tastes,
  in their apathy, their rutted, conforming life-styles.

One indication of stunted Christianity
    within many churches
  is the popular need for *sensual* experience.
If the church or the pastor pushes something

that fails to produce good feelings
and preaches about the cost of discipleship
or the Christian's responsibility
for the poor and oppressed of this society,
many so-called Christians turn off—and drop out—
and go looking for a religion that pampers and comforts
rather than provokes and challenges.
The need for sensual experience is a natural need;
Christians need mountaintop moments in their lives.
Unfortunately, they often become the focus and goal
of people's lives and eventually the substitute
for the real thing.

Another factor that results in a shallow, stunted faith
is the reach for a *materialistic* Christianity.
People can't visualize or understand a spiritual God
so, like the ancient Israelites,
they erect golden calves to dance around
and lean their lives upon.
This is sometimes symbolized by huge altars, plush pews,
and awesome, beautiful sanctuaries,
designed to lead people in the worship of God.
It is dramatized in the manner that many Christians
spend their money—
utilizing ninety-five cents out of the dollar
for themselves
while they piously contribute a nickel
to the extension of God's kingdom
in community and world.

A shallow faith produces a halfhearted,
half-baked Christianity—
a weak emaciate profession that is so far removed
from Christ's original call and challenge
that no relationship whatsoever
appears to exist between the two.
Much of contemporary Christianity
is a part-time spirituality
that people occasionally and conveniently
indulge in.

141

They are people who never left the Pablum diet
  to take on the meat of the Christian experience.
What, then, is the answer, the antidote,
  the cure for ineffective congregations,
  for the insipidity and emaciation of Christian lives?

The Gospel lesson presents it,
  figuratively but beautifully.
The disciples were fishing in shallow waters.
It was typical not only of their vocation
  but of their lives.
They had not yet experienced the profound depths
  of divine love and service.
Jesus came to them with the exhortation:
  "Put out into the deep and let down your nets."
"Master, we toiled all night and took nothing!"
  was Peter's response.
This has often been my response
  to the command and demands of Christ.
I have honestly tried to serve Him,
  to extend God's kingdom,
  to witness to my community,
  to bring Christ to people.
So often it seems to come to naught.
The disciples in the Gospel lesson incident obeyed Christ.
As a consequence of their obedience,
  their launching out into deeper waters,
  two boats were sinking under the weight
    of the netted fish.
The incident did not mean so much to the disciples
  at that time.
After Christ's resurrection, however,
  when this act was repeated,
  they began to realize
  Christ's real meaning and purpose
  for the miracle in question.
During their Lord's pre-resurrection teaching,
  their loyalty and allegiance to Him
  was sensualistic and materialistic.

143

They tried to make Him their earthly king.
They coveted His power to perform astounding miracles.
They fantasized about how they would assist Him
    in ruling over Israel.
They were confining themselves to the things
    they could see and feel and understand.
They were shortsighted, halfhearted, potted Christians.

"Put out into the deep," Jesus would say to me today.
"Get out of the shallow waters
    of the apparent and the tangible
    and push out into the depths of My reality.
You have been dangling your toes,
    just getting your feet wet,
    at the shoreline of God's great sea of grace.
Now put out into the deep and let down your nets.
Soon you will be catching men."
Maybe I am still fishing in shallow waters.
I may still be a potted, stunted, ineffective Christian.
The diagnosis of this malady is twofold.
First, *I have not really laid claim*
    to all that God through Christ has done on my behalf.
My sins have been forgiven.
I have been redeemed, reconciled to God,
    adopted as His son, and restored
    to a right relationship with my Creator
    and His design and destiny for my life.
I have, by virtue of God's promises,
    access to everything I need,
    spiritually and materially,
    to make me a bountiful servant,
    an effective minister
    in the love and service of God.
But like money in the bank,
    it isn't applicable until I cash in on it—
    claim it—use it—act as if it is so.
My weaknesses, anxieties, fears,
    hang-ups and entrapments
    are mine only because I have not laid claim

to my Father's deliverance
and accepted His liberating grace.
I have been merely existing within my foolish feelings
when I should be living freely, victoriously, joyfully
by faith in what God through Christ has done for me.
Second, *I have not yet placed myself in total commitment*
in that place where He can work in and through me.
The measure in which I recognize and embrace
what God has done for me
determines the measure in which I give of myself
to Him and His purposes
in and through service to my fellow beings.
It is obvious to me that I still have a long way to go
to be what God intends that I be in my arena
of faith and servitude.

Trouble, sorrow, sickness, weakness—human sinfulness—
beset me on all sides.
They constitute the facts of human nature
and its environment.
They are things I must deal with;
I cannot, however, deal effectively with them
in the shallow waters of my own efforts and endeavors.
"We toiled all night and took nothing!" said Simon.
The miracle-working Christ comes to me through the Word
and the Sacrament with the injunction:
"Put out into the deep and let down your nets."
It isn't very logical
It is the Master speaking; my God is commanding.
And even in the command is the promise of fulfillment.
One cannot plunge from shore to open depths
without first entering the shallows.
Shallow waters are necessary but are meant to be
the means that lead to greater depths,
never an end in themselves.
The distressing things about me,
the incapabilities within me,
all must be recognized and experienced.
I need not, however, settle for them

or be overcome by them.
"Put out into the deep and let down your nets."
It means that I get unpotted,
   that I untie the taproot of my life
   and send it deep into the grace of God.
Taking a good look at my insufficiences and weaknesses,
   I need only to abide in the fact of God's reality
   and the promise that His grace was sufficient,
   that His strength is made perfect in my weakness.
When I do this, I will discover that my nets, my life,
   will be filled with the supernatural abundance
      of God's infinite riches;
   and I shall learn how to channel this abundance
   into the empty, poverty-stricken lives of others.

My Place in the Sun

Luke 16:1-9

A marginal note on a sermon manuscript
  of a certain preacher read:
  "Weak point—shout like hell!"
I don't write such notes on my manuscripts,
  but I must admit to often feeling like this
  concerning my sermons, my ministry,
    and my life in general.
This wasn't true in the initial years of my ministry.
The student years, followed by my triumphal entry
  into a disjointed world
  as God's special envoy
  with a message of grace and judgment,
  were in many ways particularly gratifying.
I had been sheltered in parsonages
  and schools of theology.
I was convinced that I had the answers
  to most of what was wrong with humanity.

I wasn't out of manse and ivory-tower for very long
  before I discovered "weak points"—
  the alcoholic I couldn't reach,
  the marital breakdowns I couldn't mend,
  the mental and emotional distortions I couldn't fathom,
  the sicknesses I couldn't heal,
  and some of my own problems I couldn't solve.
My recitation of Bible verses,
  my fervent prayers and well-worded exhortations,
  cast as much light on these real-life problems
  as do fireflies on a foggy night.
On the one hand, my study of the New Testament
  had led me to focus on some very high
  and sometimes unrealistic standards
  in respect to the role of the minister.
I, like any Christian, was endued with divine power.

147

I was expected to reflect the attributes of Christ
   and to manifest something of His power
   amidst the chaos of this world.
I was supposed to be a sort of "little Christ"
   destined to bring a bit of heaven's power and provision
   into the weaknesses and emptiness
   of this distraught society.
On the other side of the ledger—the debit side—
   were the all-too-apparent weaknesses
      and insufficiencies of my human nature.
Instead of reflecting Christ,
   I reflected or portrayed many of my own distortions,
   or some false and faulty image
   utilized to window-dress the real "me."
Rather than manifesting divine power,
   I often "shouted like hell"
   in order to convince myself
   of the promise and existence of God's power,
   and I wrestled with doubts as to my own
      calling and significance
   as a person as well as a minister
   to problematic people.

I am no longer nearly so ambitious.
I do not aspire to be a bishop
   and only occasionally wish
   to be author of a best-seller.
I am not quite so alarmed about my inability
   to move masses or influence multitudes.
I am not ready to throw in the towel every time I fail
   to enlighten the dark path of some groping soul.
I still have bouts with discouragement,
   and there are failures from time to time,
   but I believe that I am finding "my place in the sun"
   in being what God would have me to be right where I am,
   an adequate husband and father, a loving neighbor,
   and a help-giving friend to people who cross my path.
I have a measure of peace and contentment
   that will keep me, I hope,

from becoming a frantic, grasping pursuer
    of prestige and position.
It may even resolve into a more serene life
    of power and purpose.

I am not sure what all this has to do
    with this Gospel lesson.
I have never been certain
    as to what Christ was attempting to say
    in the presentation of this parable.
It is probably a very earthy way of illustrating
    the need of a Christian to dedicate his or her life
    to making the right kind of investments
    through intelligent and Spirit-guided stewardship
    of the gifts that God has entrusted to him or her,
    intimating that if these are used
    to meet the needs of others,
    then when the time comes
    that the Christian will be in need,
    those gifts will be returned a hundredfold.
Jesus was certainly not suggesting
    that Christians today follow the example
    of the dishonest steward of the parable
    in respect to the way in which he made such investments,
    but was pointing out a measure of wisdom
    in the determination of this man
    to find himself a niche,
    "a place in the sun" for his life.
In reality, everyone has sought or is seeking for this.
The screaming hullabaloo, the beating of the air
    on every block and in every street,
    is in essence the desperate attempts of people
    to find for themselves "a place in the sun."
The distortions, the emotional and mental illnesses
        prominent in so many personalities
    may be due in part to the inability of these individuals
        to find such a place
The good news of the Gospel is that God has not left
    His children in the dark concerning their destiny;

150

He has taken great pains to reveal
what is His creatures' purpose in life.

My purpose for life, or my "place in the sun,"
is revealed largely in the very nature of God Himself.
I was made in the image of God.
Whatever that may mean, it becomes a crucial link
between the purpose of my God
and my destiny as His redeemed creature.
To discover the reason for my existence,
I must know something of God's nature
in relationship to this world,
and His plan and purpose within that relationship.

First of all, God is Creator.
He not only created the world, He continues to create it.
He continues to operate in and through the ongoing order,
expressing Himself in manifold and wondrous ways.
He has not left the world to its own whims
but constantly seeks to work out His creative purposes
in and throughout the world.
Second, God is Redeemer.
Though God's creatures rebelled against their Creator,
plunging all of humanity into chaotic disharmony,
God in His mercy seeks to woo and win His creatures
back to Himself.
He reveals Himself to humankind in Jesus Christ.
Man and woman could never measure up
to God's righteous standards,
so God in Christ fulfilled them in their stead,
bearing the guilt and consequences
of humanity's rebellion
in order that God's children
might be reconciled to Him.
Third, God is Holy Spirit.
It is by His Spirit
that He perpetually manifests Himself
in the fellowship of men and women
who make up the body of Christ
and who are seeking to advance His kingdom in the world.

Within that fellowship He unites and guides,
   impells and empowers,
   and thereby carries out His purposes,
   all pointing toward that great event
   when the divine kingdom will be consummated
   and the eternal and almighty God revealed fully
   to His faithful and loving children.

Because I am made in the image of God,
   I am meant to be *creative*.
I have been given the high privilege of being
   a co-laborer with Him
   in the task of restoring the universe
   in accordance with His plan.
It is this that gives dignity and purpose to the work
   of containing rivers to utilize their power
   and harnassing the sun's rays to produce energy,
   of preserving our environment,
   of supporting the efforts of science
   to bring safety and security to humankind,
   healing to crippled bodies,
   and quality and dignity, freedom and justice,
   to people of all races and classes.
I am to be creative.

Because I am created in the image of God,
   I am, by His grace and direction, to be *redemptive*.
This has to do with my interpersonal relationships,
   the way I respond to the needs of my fellow persons.
As Christ loved me, and through His redemptive love
   and His conequential death on the cross
   made a way of salvation for me,
   so I am to "love others to Christ."
It is for this reason that Christians are freed from sin
      and reconciled to God—
   that they might serve their neighbors.
I have become a channel and vehicle
   for Christ's redeeming love
   into the lives of others about me.
As God reached me through others,

so He chooses to relate to and draw others
into His redeeming love through me.
I am to be redemptive—
    or an instrument of God's redemption—
    in my relationship to others.

Because I am created in the image of God,
    He expects that I manifest Him
    in *channeling His Spirit* to others
    in home, community, and world.
Working in harmony with other members of Christ's body,
    I am a tool, an instrument, a vehicle of God's Spirit
    in the building of His kingdom on this planet,
    for the recruiting of others,
    drawing others into His saving grace
    and into contact with the divine power
    that will redeem and empower them
        for purposeful living.

Thus I have found my place in the sun.
It is here—right where I am.
It includes joys and sorrows, successes and defeats,
    bright moments and dark hours.
It demands obedience and loyalty
    to my Creator and Redeemer.
It relies upon the empowering and motivating
    of His ever-present Spirit.
It promises the satisfaction and enrichment
    of meaningful life and service
This is my place in the sun.

King of the Hill

Luke 18:9-14

One of my favorite games in the rough and tumble years
  of my childhood was what we called "king of the hill."
The biggest kid in the gang
  would take his place on some knoll
  and challenge all oncomers to dethrone him—
  which four or five of us promptly proceeded to do.
Then one of us would take his place
  and repeat the challenge.

This is not peculiar to childhood.
There is in most people the insatiable desire
  to be "king of the hill."
Many strive until the very end of their lives
  to be king of some hill or other—
  to be the best writer, artist, musician, chess player,
  skater, high-jumper—or to achieve some record
  in the number of miles they can run
  or goldfish they can swallow—or whatever.
There is, it appears,
  a need to discover personal identity,
  and one of the bizarre ways of seeking it
  is to bury one's inferiority feelings
  in some kind of achievement
  that makes that person "king of the hill"
  in a particular phase or facet of life.

There is one vice of which no person is free.
People may readily admit they are bad-tempered
    or self-centered,
  but few will accuse themselves of this vice.
It is the sin of pride, which sometimes shows up
  in the temptation or endeavor
  to be "king of the hill."
It is the central and basic evil
  within a person's nature.

154

It was through pride that the devil became the devil.
It is pride that leads to most other vices.
Other vices may even bring people together.
One may find good fellowship and friendliness
   among drunken or unchaste people,
   but pride always resolves in enmity—
   not only between people, but between people and God.

It is represented in this Gospel lesson in Jesus' parable
   in the character of the Pharisee in the temple.
It is a picture of a man who is satisfied with himself
   and, as such, a man who under such circumstances
   can never meet God.
If there is anything that can short-circuit
   a Christian's joy and vibrant witness,
   it is this vice straight from hell spiritual pride
It shows up often in my life—
   particularly in my attitudes toward others.
Rather than broadcast the good points or traits
      of my friends or foes,
   I tend to pick out flaws and weaknesses.
While I may say unkind things about others,
   I withdraw in horror if I hear an unkind word
      about myself.
While I may look down my nose at those people
      who are participating
   in things which I think are sinful,
   I may, at the same time, be allowing greater evils
   to exist in my own life—such as judging others,
   gossiping, bigotry or prejudice,
   or apathy and neglect concerning my fellow persons.

This Gospel lesson frames up another picture.
While the Pharisee was smugly satisfied with himself,
   putting himself above all those around him,
   a little man in the corner, a publican,
   one who had no thought about anyone else
      at this moment,
   one who was utterly dissatisfied with himself,
   in sorrow over his sins, his failures and flaws,

with despair in his soul smote his breast and said,
"God, be merciful to me a sinner!"
What a vast difference between these two characters!
As far apart as the poles of pride and humility
   are the spirits of these two men.
The point is, two men came to the temple that day,
   but only one met God.
It was the one who came in humility,
   seeing nobody's failures but his own,
   with no bones to pick or axe to grind
   concerning anybody else.

He came to get right in his own heart with God.
"I tell you," said Jesus,
   "this man went down to his house justified
      rather than the other;
   for every one who exalts himself will be humbled,
   but he who humbles himself will be exalted."

How can I be sure of meeting God
   in my worship and prayers?
I must come to Him for the purpose of meeting Him.
Only then can I expect to be prepared to meet Him,
   to receive His comfort and counsel,
   His exhortations and admonitions.
I must come cognizant of life's labors and burdens.
"Come unto Me, all who labor and are heavy laden,
   and I will give you rest," said Jesus.
The people Jesus effectively dealt with
   in His earthly sojourn
   were people who had burdens, problems,
   and who cried to Him for help.
People must sometimes be awakened
   from their numbing lethargy,
   the anesthetic sleep of this world,
   before they can realize any need for divine help.
I must come poverty-stricken,
   utterly devoid of personal merits
   or self-righteousness.

I must get down off the hill
   where I am trying to be king
   and come in dire need.
"Nothing in my hand I bring, simply to Thy cross I cling,"
   wrote the hymn writer.
I must come to receive that which I cannot find
   in myself or in anyone else.
My immediate concern
   is not the needs of others at this point
   but rather healing for my own sickness,
   my desperate need for divine grace.
I must come as a sinner seeking always the undeserved,
   unmerited mercy of a loving God.
"God, be merciful to me a sinner!"
I must come with the desire and the willingness
   to be reconciled to God *and* my fellow persons.
This is possible only if I come acknowledging
   and confessing my sins to God—
   and to the people I have hurt.
I must come in the attitude of total commitment
   and the determination, by God's grace,
   to obey God and to carry out His purposes
   whatever the cost or the consequences.
While one's degree of commitment enlarges
   as he or she continues to walk with God,
   even the initial coming and the perpetual comings
   must include the desire and willingness
   to follow Jesus Christ at all costs.

There is only one sure way to meet God.
I must come down off my hill,
   take off the frills and fancy dress,
   tear down the facades, strip away the camouflage,
   and come humbly before Him.
This transition, this changeover,
   this journey from pride to humility,
   is made by way of confession.
I must dare to say,
   "The blame for my failure and wrongdoing is mine;

I have disobeyed God; I have hurt others."
And then, if I, like the publican of the parable,
   am to return to my place justified,
   I must receive by faith God's word
     of absolute forgiveness,
   recognizing that God through Christ *has* received me
   and pardoned me and enrobed me in His righteousness.

I need no longer to be king of some hill or other.
I am the ordained and adopted son and servant of God.

The Master's Touch

Mark 7:31-37

Christians have heard
  and probably subscribe to the statement
  that God can change the world through them.
It is doubtful that many of them really believe it.
Nevertheless, it is true.
They may further contemplate the fact that this is
  . the only way in which God can change the world.
God came to this world through the human Christ.
This world's creatures would have no other way
  of knowing and experiencing the love of God
  save through God-incarnate, Jesus Christ,
  and through His followers
  who communicated His life and message,
  love and power,
    to those who crossed their paths.
One may sense something of the power of God
    in the thundering surf
  or His beauty in the magnificent rose,
  but His love reaches people
  through the words and deeds of human flesh.
The tangible and human Christ
  is no longer on this planet.
In His place is the presence
  of the invisible Spirit of God,
  who is clothed in the hearts and minds and bodies
  of His children who abide in this disjointed world.
Therefore the only way
  in which the love of the heavenly Father
  can be transmitted to the love-starved,
  hate-ridden, poverty-stricken masses
    of this fractured world
  is by way of His sons and daughters, his servants,
  who have been touched by His reconciling love
  and whose lives in turn

reflect and demonstrate that love
to their fellow persons about them.

Jesus never took a course in psychology
and never participated in
the kind of touch-therapy experiments
that fascinate the populace today.
Yet this was the method by which He healed the deaf-mute
of this Gospel lesson.
He took the man aside, away from the crowd,
"put His fingers into his ears,
and He spat and touched his tongue."

The physical touch is important to infants and children.
Those who are denied the physical touch of human love,
expressed in care and cuddling, affection and concern,
often grow up severely distorted or impaired
in their lives and personalities.
Now it is generally accepted that the need for love
expressed in physical touching
is not restricted to children
but continues throughout all of life.
God continues to touch His children with love,
to assure, to give strength and courage and joy,
through the laying on of hands, the water of Baptism,
the bread and wine of the Eucharist.
He speaks to His children through the printed Word
of the Bible and the proclamations of His ministers.
His most common way of touching
earth's creatures and thereby revealing
His love and concern for them, however,
is by way of the hands,
the touches and embraces, the smiles and tears,
the human expressions of love
from His sons and daughters within the human family.

This Gospel lesson reveals one small glimpse
of the miracle-working touch of the Lord and Master.
The hidden, slumbering power of the Old Testament
bursts forth into life through the touch of Jesus,

God come to earth.
By His touch eyes were made to see, ears to hear,
   tongues to speak, feet to walk, hands to move.
By His touch even the dead were made to live again.
But His touch was to mean far more than that,
   for He came not to touch head and hands and feet only,
   but the hearts of men and women.
He came to disentangle those broken strands of life,
   those discordant harmonies
   of fear and despair and hopelessness.
He came that by His miraculous touch men and women
   might again be brought into a right relationship
   with their Creator-God and walk once more
   within His orbit for their lives.
The New Testament stands as a living, pulsating,
   vibrant monument and witness
   to the power of God's touch—
   not only in tongues set free to speak, ears to hear,
      eyes to see, feet to walk,
   but far more in lives that were set free
      from the bondage of sin
   to sing and to live praises unto God.
A woman was taken in adultery and dragged before Jesus
   to be judged.
By His touch she became a loyal and loving disciple.
A tax collector turned from his cheating and robbing
   to feel His touch and become a follower of Christ.
A hater of Christians who sought them out
   for imprisonment or execution
   felt the touch of Christ
   and was transformed from the cruelest persecutor
   into the greatest propagator of Christianity
   that the world has ever known.
And things like this are happening every day
   throughout this world.
It seldom makes headlines, but alcoholics, drug addicts,
   criminals, sick, lonely, empty, suicidal people
   are being touched by the Spirit of God and transformed
   into His loving and serving sons and daughters.

163

The touch of Christ—what can it do for me?
It *obliterates the sins and failures of the past.*
It may not wipe out all the consequences
   of these wrongdoings; old wounds heal very slowly.
However, it cleanses out the guilt,
   and removes the condemnation
   enrobes me in the perfect goodness
      and righteousness of Christ,
   and presents me before God
   just as if those ugly things had never happened.
The touch of Christ heals me forever from the sickness
   of my past sin and self-centeredness.
   and it is His continued touch
   that will transform present and future selfishness
   into greater, deeper, larger experiences
   of self-giving, self-sacrificing love for others.

The touch of Christ *sets me free*
   from the bondages and enslavements of this existence
   in order to prepare and challenge me
   to prepare others for life everlasting.
I am free to die.
I do not seek this ultimate earthly experience,
   and I may be apprehensive at times about that untried
   and unknown event I must eventually face;
   but I am free from its terror and unafraid to die.
Because I have lost my fear of death
   I am free to live—and to love—
   to risk life and possessions in my efforts
   to touch others with healing, joy-giving love.
"I have been crucified with Christ," wrote Paul;
   "it is no longer I who live, but Christ who lives in me;
   and the life I now live . . . I live by faith
      in the Son of God,
   who loved me and gave Himself for me."
Christ's touch not only sets me free from sin
   but frees me from its bondages and compulsions
   which cheat me out of all that God has made
      available to me.

I am set free from the "dos" and "don'ts"
    of man-made moralities.
I am set free from the innumerable fears
    that plague and cripple my life.
    Thus the touch of Christ enables me to truly live—
    above the fleeting realities about me
        even while I dwell among them.

The touch of Christ *gives me inner security.*
The human personality simply cannot stand
    living in an empty, meaningless universe.
It will eventually go to pieces.
I am secure—not because everything always makes sense—
    but because I belong to God
    and am on this world by God's design
    and all things do eventually work together for good
    for those who love God and live according to His purposes.

The touch of Christ
    brings plan and purpose to my life.
While I do not receive a blueprint
    for my future in this world,
    I do follow a divine Leader who has a plan,
    a design and destiny for me.
I am not just aimlessly beating the air
    as are so many who live apart from God;
    I am a servant of the living God.
I represent Him in my world today.
I am dedicated to His purposes and objectives,
    and this gives meaning and significance to my life.

The touch of Christ *gives me true identity.*
I *am* somebody.
Whatever my upbringing or present circumstances,
    my weaknesses or distortions,
    I am significant
"Thou hast made him little less than God,"
    gasped David as he contemplated man and woman
    amidst the wonders of creation.
My name is Christian.

165

God has given me His Spirit to live within me.
He has made me His temple to indwell,
 His child to be His heir,
 His disciple through whom to serve,
 His own to love forever.
Truly, I have found my identity
 in this remarkable touch of Jesus Christ.

How did this touch of Christ come upon me?
It came in the presence of His Holy Spirit.
The Holy Spirit came through my baptism.
"Repent and be baptized . . . and you shall receive
 the gift of the Holy Spirit," said Peter.
It became real to me when I decisively and willfully
 committed myself to the Christ of the baptismal covenant.
This did not resolve in the dissolving of all my problems
 or the irradication of all my conflicts,
 but with Christ's touch came a new order and harmony
 and joy and power and meaning and purpose into my life.
God grant that it will resolve in the extending of my life
 into the unbearable, unendurable, conflicts
  of others about me,
 where I may become the loving and healing touch
  of God upon their lives.

And Who Is My Neighbor?

Luke 10:25-37

The parable of this Gospel lesson was presented by Jesus
   in response to a lawyer who wanted to know
   how he could be certain of heaven and eternal life
    for himself.
"What is written in the Law?" asked Jesus.
"You shall love the Lord your God
   with all your heart,
   and with all your soul,
   and with all your strength,
   and with all your mind;
   and your neighbor as yourself,"
    responded the lawyer.
"You have answered right," said Jesus;
   "do this, and you will live."
The lawyer wasn't about to challenge
   the old and revered commandment,
   but he was cagy and yet remarkably honest
   in asking the question, "And who is my neighbor?"

I don't know if Jesus' answer
   was a surprise to the lawyer,
   but I do know it to be
    a revealing and judgmental condemnation
   upon much that goes on
    in the name of Christianity today.
The lawyer knew that no ordinary person could challenge
   his love for God.
After all, he said the right words,
   went through the required motions,
   lived within the principles and precepts
    of his religion,
   and carried on a very respectable kind of life.
But the second half of the commandment—love of neighbors—
   stopped him cold.

167

That was where the authenticity of his faith
   could be challenged.
He had only one recourse: "And who is my neighbor?"

It is Jesus' answer to the lawyer,
   the story of the Good Samaritan,
   that tends to make much of my professed
      and assumed piety,
   and the professions of scores of church people,
   somewhat unbelievable and disturbingly inadequate.
As long as I say the right words
   and belong to the right church,
   my faith can hardly be disproved by mortal man.
The "love your neighbor" aspect
   of the Great Commandment, however,
   drives me against the wall.
I am reluctant to confront the import
   of Jesus' response to the Lawyer's question
   because it presents a challenge that may reveal
   the authencity or phoniness of my faith.
I have recognized the importance
   of preaching to my neighbor,
   of trying to lead him or her
   to the place of conversion,
   which, incidentally, the Good Samaritan
      of Jesus' parable never did,
   but I have interpreted
      the "love your neighbor" injunction
   in ways that allow me to indulge
   in what may be a very questionable faith.
I know my salvation is from God.
I must accept as a gift God's love for me
   as it is demonstrated and proclaimed by Jesus Christ.
I cannot earn that love; it already exists.
I can only accept it—or refuse to accept it.
It is when I truly accept it
   that I become a channel and communicator
   of divine love toward my neighbor.
It isn't enough for me to say the right words like

"I love You, Jesus," or "I accept You, Christ."
There must be a total commital,
   a placing of myself at God's disposal,
   "presenting my body as a living sacrifice."
This is not mere words; it is an *act*.
The only way I can *act* as a loving child and servant
   of the invisible God is to commit myself
   to the needs of my visible neighbor.
If I do not do this, something is wrong with my faith.

Thus my faith is challenged today,
   and I fall back on the same question
      projected by the lawyer
   of our Gospel lesson parable:
   "And who is my neighbor?"
"Who *is* my neighbor?"
Lonely senior citizens in rest homes
      throughout my community,
   deserted wives with children under their feet
      and Mother-Hubbard cupboards,
   the couple breaking up next door,
   the alcoholic down the block,
   the minority-race family
      that just moved in on X Avenue,
   the teen-agers who smoke pot and steal hubcaps,
   the millions throughout my world who are oppressed,
      deprived, disinherited, hungry, poverty-stricken—
   these are my neighbors.
God's command is to *love* them—
   not with sentimental words
   but with Christ-impelled actions.

I remember the story of John the Baptizer,
   the forerunner and introducer of Jesus Christ,
   who emerged from the wilderness
   to prepare the people for Christ's coming.
He blasted away at the crowds
   attracted to this remarkable prophet from the past
   with severe denunciations
   of their hypocrisy and fruitlessness.

They had faithfully performed their religious exercises
  and had clung proudly to their traditions but,
  according to John the Baptizer,
  had about as much chance of becoming
    a part of God's kingdom
  as a dead fruit tree had of escaping the axe.
They were stripped naked under his scathing condemnations
  and were frightened by his proclamations.
"What then shall we do?" they exclaimed.
John's reply was simple and to the point:
  "He who has two coats,
  let him share with him who has none."

"It's all right to talk about long white robes
      over yonder . . ."
  said Martin Luther King Jr.
  in the last sermon he preached
  before his assassination.
"But all too many people need
  some suits and dresses and shoes
  to wear down here.
It's all right to talk about streets
  flowing with milk and honey.
But God has commanded us
  to be concerned about the slums down here
  and the children who can't eat
  three square meals a day.
It's all right to talk about the New Jerusalem,
  but one day God's creatures must talk about
  the new New York, the new Atlanta,
  the new Philadelphia, the new Los Angeles,
  the new Memphis, Tennessee."

"Which of these three," Jesus asked the lawyer,
  "do you think proved neighbor to the man
  who fell among the robbers?"
"The one who showed mercy on him," he responded.
And Jesus said to him: "Go and do likewise."
This is, in essence, what Jesus is saying
  to His church and to me today.

171

Some people call it the social gospel,
   but enough evidence has been presented to indicate
   that it is an important part of Christ's message.

"Go and do likewise."
Do it through denominational structures
   that can reach out to the needs of the masses
   throughout the world.
Do it through social and political structures
   that by means of educational, welfare,
   mental health, and medical organizations
   can touch the needs of people
   in this nation and its crowded cities.
Do it through the local congregation
   that can zero in on specific projects and needs
   in its own community.
Do it through the personal touch
   where every committed Christian
   as a servant and minister
   will reach out in love to others around him or her
   and through human love and concern,
   empowered and inspired by God's love,
   hopefully and ultimately introduce them
   to the redeeming love of Jesus Christ.

It is time that I worry less about my own salvation,
   my security or peace of mind,
   and become more concerned about obeying God.
He has taken care of my salvation;
   heaven is my eternal home.
In the meantime, He has a job for me to carry out
   in this fractured world—
   the Good Samaritan task of loving my neighbor
   and of dramatizing that love at the point
   of his or her immediate need.
"Go and do likewise."

Rise Up and Live!

Luke 7:11-17

This Gospel lesson deals with Christ's confrontation
   with human grief and the event of death
   and with His power to overcome both grief and death.
It is designed to assure God's children
   of such power in respect to their lives
   and irradicate once and for always
   their fear of this ultimate event.
The fact is that I am not likely
   to be of much use to God
   until my eventual exodus from this world,
   though fraught with apprehension,
   holds no real fear for me.
Death is a part of the mystery of life—
   one single event in the whole panorama of eternity.
It is a single step from the front stoop
   of this three-dimensional world
   into the living room of everlasting union with God—
   one that Christians may well anticipate
   but certainly need not fear.

This fantastic miracle may also be applied
   to other kinds of dying—
   those that affect one's spiritual life,
   the church, the Christian group,
   and the relationship and responsibility
   to neighbor and world.
It is possible to be dead even while one is alive.
This is the death that characterizes
   those who are outside of Christ—
   even those who fool themselves
   into believing they are really "living it up"
   and all the time are dead
   to the great gifts of God's loving grace.

They are out of joint with God,
   out of His orbit for their lives,
   and have never truly awakened or come to life—
   the life of purpose and joy
   revealed through Jesus Christ.
Then there is that kind of death or dying
   which characterizes some Christians.
Whatever the reason,
   frustration, fear, pride, depression,
   inability to understand
   or unwillingness to commit themselves
   to the whole life and will of Christ,
   they turn off to the world,
   pull in their nerve-endings,
   and refuse to or neglect to become involved
   in the struggles of humanity about them.
Though confessing Christians,
   these people separate themselves from the world,
   for they are convinced that the world is going to hell.
They pull apart into little clubs or cults
   that shield them from the world
   and its ugly, agonizing problems.
They cannot love the suffering, oppressed, addicted,
   enslaved, hate-ridden people about them.
And John, the evangelist, once said
   that if one can't love,
   then he or she is already dead.
These people are assured that they are ready for heaven—
   and are eagerly awaiting the trumpet call
   that will announce Christ's final advent—
   but their salvation has never set them free
   to live joyfully and fruitfully in a revolutionary world
   and lovingly risk and sacrifice for humanity about them.

This death and dying also touches and tempts
   many who fervently believe
   in Jesus Christ and His promises—
   even those who accept His commission
   to evangelize the world—

but who are doing more crying
over personal doubts and fears,
inadequacies and failures,
than they are claiming and living
by God's provision and power.
I know that I am often frightened by the world
and what transpires about me—
and tempted, at times,
to throw up my hands in despair.
It is a temptation, as well, to give up on this planet
and to use the church as a port in the storm
rather than a launching pad
for dynamic living and serving
in this broken world.
When I allow this to happen, however,
then I may also be in the process of dying,
of losing out on the abundant life
that God through Christ has made available to me.

The message of this Gospel lesson—
whether it be to those who are afraid to die,
to those who are still outside of God's saving grace,
or to any of God's children who may be gradually dying
under the pressures and pains of difficult circumstances
within this uncertain and insecure world—
is, "I say to you, arise."

In Jesus' contact with the atrocious fact of death,
I see, first of all, *compassion manifested.*
"And when the Lord saw her [the mother of the deceased],
He had compassion on her and said to her,
'Do not weep.'"
Jesus portrays no respect nor mercy for death itself,
nor for humankind's sin and disobedience
which constitutes its origin.
Nor does He try in any way to cover up the fact
that this world's sojourn
will be full of sorrow and pain,
contradiction and conflict.
Jesus comes to listen, understand, forgive, heal—

but also to convict of sin and challenge His followers
  to leave the state of dying, this spiritual sickness
  that afflicts God's children, and rise up and live.
"Do not weep," He is saying to doubting, grasping,
  rebelling, complaining Christians today:
  "You have nothing to complain about—
  save your sins which I have forgiven;
  stop crying—rise up and live."
He speaks not in anger, but in loving compassion.
God understands and seeks to absolve the fear
  and bear the burdens of His children
  and impart to them the grace to stand firm and true
  against their many conflicts.
This grace is apparent, however, only when Christians
  rise up and live, when they lay claim to live
  by God's promises and provision
  and began to act in their daily lives
  on the premise that such promises are true
  and such provision has been granted.

I see in the miracle of this Gospel lesson
  the fact of *death arrested.*
"And He came and touched the bier,
  and the bearers stood still."
There is nothing miraculous about the touch alone,
  but this simple act is a remarkable symbol
  of Jesus' glorious purpose for coming to this planet
  and His continual presence with His church
    through His Spirit.
It was His task, and it is now the task of His followers,
  to stop the bleeding, to alleviate the suffering,
  to command the bearers who are carrying
  people's helpless bodies and souls into perdition
  to stand still.
He did this with those who came to Him.
I must reach out to do this,
  in His name and by His grace,
  with the bleeding, suffering people
    who cross my path.

177

The final picture of this Gospel lesson
   is that of *life transmitted*.
"Young man, I say to you, arise!" were the words of Jesus.
Rise up and live! He is saying to me
   and all of God's beloved children today.
The process of dying and death can be cut short
   only by the influx of new life.
"For as the Father raises the dead and gives them life,
   so also the Son gives life to whom He will. . . .
I came that they may have life, and have it abundantly,"
      said Jesus at other times.
Not only is He a compassionate Savior,
   nor does His work cease with death's arrest,
   but He holds out the offer of everlasting life.
"Even when we were dead through our trespasses . . ."
   wrote Paul,
   "God made [us] alive together with Him,
   having forgiven us all our trespasses."
If my life tends to be dull and deadening,
   or if I am more often crying or complaining
      than I am rejoicing,
   it may be that I am still a dying Christian.
I still haven't learned how to live,
   how to lay hold of that love and life made available
   through Jesus Christ, a life that even in the midst
   of doubt and pain and insecurity   ·
   is a life of peace and joy.

It is one thing to know
   that my relationship to God is secure.
I know this because Jesus is my Savior and Lord.
It is quite another to accept my assignment
   in God's world as His son and servant,
   to love the world He created,
   and to truly and joyfully live for and love and serve
   my brothers and sisters in the human family.
This power, this life, all that I need
   to live a joyful, effective, abundant life,
   is within me.

It has been granted.
I need only to accept it,
    and to live and act as if it is so—
    whether I *feel* it or not.
Only then will I discover
    love and joy and meaning and purpose
    and begin to infect others about me
    with the contagion of God's life and Spirit.

God help me,
    and His sons and daughters
        throughout this world,
    to rise up and live!

The Incomparable Experience

Matthew 9:1-8

A prophet out of the Old Testament
    puts a well-phrased question
    to the inhabitants of the twentieth century:
    "Why do you spend your money for that
        which is not bread,
    and your labor for that
        which does not satisfy?"
It ends with a question mark that curls itself
    around the confused lives of millions
        throughout the world today.
There are multitudes of people
    who live only for pleasure.
Their creed is, "Eat, drink, be merry."
There are others who try to cram their lives with gadgets,
    only to eventually discover that "a man's life
    does not consist in the abundance of his possessions."
What do men and women need and want most of all?
What do people really hunger for?

The poet Robert Browning put the answer into verse:
    "O God, where do they tend, these struggling aims?
    What could I have? What is the 'sleep' which seems
    To bound all: Can there be a 'waking' point
    Of crowning life? . . .
    The last point I can trace is—rest beneath
    Some better essense than itself, in weakness;
    This is 'myself,' not what I think should be:
    And what is that I hunger for but God?"
Studdert-Kennedy wrote:
    "Peace with God is the one absolute necessity
    of the fully human life; it is the plain bread
    which every soul must have in order to live. . . ."

This Gospel lesson refers to that bread
for which every persons longs,
that which can come from God alone.
The paralytic was brought to Christ for healing.
He found the healing he came for,
but he found something he had
never dared to anticipate,
the need of which he may
not even have recognized.
By means of the divine touch of God this man was delivered
not only from the paralysis which crippled his body,
but he was delivered from that paralysis
which stifled his soul.
Though he may not have immediately realized
its full significance,
he in that hour came upon
the incomparable experience of forgiveness,
an experience which resolved
in his restoration to God.
He was reunited to the heavenly Father,
reinstated in the heavenly Father's purposes.
"Take heart, My son," said Jesus;
"your sins are forgiven."

Most people have some awareness
of the joy of restoration.
I will never forget the new light in a child's eyes
when that child, after his or her crime and punishment,
was completely restored to the parent's arms
and affections again.
I doubt that there is any experience on a human level
so warm and real as that of restoration
to the love and devotion of mate or sweetheart
after some senseless spat.
In their search for happiness in kicks and thrills,
wealth or pleasure, the pathetic inhabitants
of this chaos-ridden planet
have little inkling of the fact
that the incomparable experience of life

is found in a person's restoration to,
acceptance by, and forgiveness from God.

When I come to the point of realizing
    that all is not well between God and me,
    that there are disorders and failures in my life,
    that sin and disobedience are obscuring
        my relationship with God,
    the first thing I must recognize is that
    the experience of forgiveness is essential.
While I am not supposing that the paralysis
    of the man brought to Jesus
    was due to a guilt complex,
    I do note that Jesus
    bypassed the disease for the moment
    and went straight to the heart
        of his necessity,
    his need for forgiveness.
It is the prime need of all humankind.
    and it is a daily need—
    this experience of forgiveness.
It is the most urgent of all humanity's cries and clamors.
The fontal source of all sorrow and suffering,
    misery and despair, is human beings' wrongdoing.
The first step in effecting a cure for humanity's ills
    is to deal with this wrongdoing,
    and this is accomplished through forgiveness
    and restoration to God.
Sin is, in effect, a person's "no" to God,
    his or her attempt to do away with God,
    a deliberate and defiant attempt to cut across
    the will and purposes of God.
The consequences are obvious throughout the world.
The one experience guaranteed to put a person
    back in God's order and orbit for his or her life
    is the incomparable experience of forgiveness.
It will not solve all of a person's problems overnight.
Neither does it promise to eradicate all the consequences
    of past sin in one's life.

Nevertheless, this experience restores a person
    to God and His purposes once more
    and thus introduces that person
    to the peace and happiness
    that is the answer to his or her deepest longings.

The second matter I need to be reminded of,
    and which is indicated by the incident
        of our Gospel lesson,
    is that *the experience of forgiveness is possible.*
Natural law is unrelenting:
    What a person sows, that shall that person reap;
    as a person acts, so that person must bear
        the consequences of such an act.
It is not surprising that the idea becomes rooted
    in many a logical mind
    that forgiveness is not possible.
The grace of God, however, slices through
    all of the condemnatory and judgmental accusations
        and pronouncements of the Law,
    and the glad news of the Gospel is
    that forgiveness is possible,
    that a person can be delivered
    from the paralysis of sin
    and be restored to God's will
    and walk within His purposes once more.
Natural law may be unrelenting,
    but God is personal Spirit and creative Love,
    and God says: "I have swept away your transgressions
    like a cloud and your sins like mist. . . .
    As far as the east is from the west,
    so far have I removed your transgressions from you."
Forgiveness by no means indicates
    that God is making light of sin.
On the contrary, God reveals the hatefulness of sin
    in the very act of cleansing it away;
    it is precisely in forgiveness
    that His inflexible righteousness appears.
It was in the hour of Christ's crucifixion

that there was introduced into the tragic fact of sin
    and its devastating consequences
a force capable of shattering
that vicious and stifling bondage
in which the human race was held fast.

A third truth so important to me in this matter is that
    the forgiveness of sin can be my experience now.
What this Gospel lesson is suggesting
    and the New Testament as a whole makes so emphatic,
    is that it isn't necessary to continue lying bound
        and helpless
    within the soul-destroying paralysis
    and power
        of unforgiven sin.
"If we confess our sins," writes John,
    "He is faithful and just,
    and will forgive our sins and cleanse us
    from all unrighteousness."
True repentance, of course, includes renunciation,
    and this refers to continuous and persistent attempts
    to turn away from sins and wrongdoings
    which betray me and come between me and God.
I fail here and must accept
    the experience of forgiveness,
    far from being a single, once-for-all experience,
    as a perpetual experience.
The state of grace is a state of life for me
    and one I must live in continually
        and return to incessantly
    by way of the cross of Jesus Christ.

Finally, *the experience of forgiveness is the basis
    yet only the beginning of the Christian life.*
Jesus said to the paralytic after he was forgiven:
    "Rise, take up your bed and go. . . ."
He said a great deal more to His disciples:
    "Go into all the world and preach the Gospel. . . .
    You did not choose Me, but I chose you
    and appointed you that you should go. . . ."

185

In spite of Jesus' numerous injunction to His disciples
   in the first as well as the twentieth century,
   so many of God's children,
   though delivered from the paralysis of sin,
   are still bound hand and foot, heart and life,
   in the paralysis of inactivity.
The forgiveness of God, that incomparable experience,
   is that which sets me free from the paralysis of sin
   in order that I might be engaged
      in eternal activity for Him.
While I continually must submit to the loving grace
   of God's forgiveness, I am commanded by Him
   to "rise, take up my bed and go . . ."
   launching out in sacrificial service
   to His creatures about me on His behalf.
Confession must be followed by commitment.
The life of a Christian,
   the blessed task of following Christ,
   is a full-time vocation.
When I embrace it as such,
   it guarantees the incomparable experience
      of forgiveness—
   no matter what my failures may be—
   and the grace and divine power that will turn
   even my failures
   into something significant
   and keep me always within the objectives
      and purposes of God.

Living in the Shadows

Luke 21:25-36

Thomas Campbell, a poet out of the last century,
  once penned these words:
    "Tis the sunset of life gives me mystical lore,
    And coming events cast their shadows before."
I am living in the shadows—
  and the gaiety, the prosperity,
  the sensuality and superficiality about me
  do not succeed in obliterating those shadows.
I have an ominous feeling that these shadows
  are prophetic harbingers of things to come.
I have always assumed that the world will not go on
  endlessly like an ever-flowing stream.
Now prophesying is no longer confined to Biblical writers
  and to preachers who paint
  lurid and frightening pictures of things to come.
Scientists, statesmen, educators are raising their voices
  in warnings of the eventual doom that awaits us.
"I see more evidence of impending doom
  on the front page of my newspaper
  than I hear about from the pulpits of our churches,"
  exclaimed one editor.

Someone once observed that "the man who is wise enough
  to discern the signs of the times is never
    caught napping
  by the swift tide of human events."
This may be what Jesus is intimating
  in this Gospel lesson—
  a sort of word to the wise
  to be aware of the shadows.
"And there will be signs
  in sun and moon and stars," He said,
  "and upon the earth distress of nations
  in perplexity at the roaring of the sea and the waves,

men fainting with fear and with foreboding
    of what is coming on the world."
God's creatures are living in the shadows.
Now, as never before, they are exhorted
    to take seriously the warning of Jesus.
"Take heed to yourselves," said the Lord,
    "lest your hearts be weighed down
    with dissipation and drunkenness and cares of this life,
    and that day come upon you suddenly like a snare. . . .
    Watch at all times, praying that you may have strength
    to escape all these things that will take place,
    and to stand before the Son of man."

"This is a day when many shake their heads and wonder
    what the world is coming to," said one pastor,
    "and others lift their heads and wonder
    at the One who comes."
The shadows indicate that the hour is late.
It strongly suggests that if this earth's creatures
    are to welcome coming events
        with expectancy rather than fear,
    as the coming dawn rather than the approaching doom,
    they had better do something about it.
For one thing, *it is high time that they find
    the way back to the fold of God,*
    that people discover or rediscover
    God's will and purpose for their lives.
Some of God's children have come across
    some interesting detours that tempted them
    to leave the King's highway.
Wide, attractive trails
    gradually dwindled into rutted tracks—
    and finally to the desert wasteland
    of the isolated and empty self.
The primary function of the church
    is to guide lost people back to the "way,"
    and Jesus said: "I am the way, and the truth,
        and the life;
    no one comes to the Father but by Me."

It is high time that those who profess His name
   and go through the forms and motions of faith
   get off the fence and make some genuine decisions
   in terms of their relationship to God.
A teacher of my youth referred to fence-sitting Christians
   as mugwamps—birds who sit on a fence,
   their "mug" on one side and their "wamp" on the other.
If they have little real assurance
   of God's love and concern
   of their preparedness for coming events,
   it may be that they have never made a clear-cut,
   full-bodied decision to accept and follow Jesus Christ.
They may be shadow-boxing with God and eternal verities,
   or playing "church" the way children play "house"
   or play at being grown-ups.
They need to commit themselves to the marriage of faith
   in the redemptive purposes of God.

It it high time that God's children get to work.
There is still time to introduce loved ones, relatives,
   friends, neighbors to the love and grace of God.
It means that Christians cease worshiping at the altars
      of materialism
   and dedicate the things they tend
      to put first in their lives back to God
   and see to it that they work for Him and His purposes.
It is time for them to cease living unto themselves,
   roll up their sleeves, and begin spending
      and expending their lives and means
   in sacrificial service for others
   in order that they might be ready
      to greet the dawn.

It is high time that those who claim
      to follow Jesus Christ
   begin to act like the Christ they presume to follow.
Scientist John-Wren once wrote:
   "I can say quite emphatically that I should never
   dream of calling myself a Christian
   unless I had become convinced

that the original Christian vision
was something utterly different from—
indeed in many ways totally opposed to—
almost everything that has passed as Christianity
for most of the church's history."
Jesus identified Himself
not with the rich and self-sufficient,
but with the poor and the suffering.
He grew up with the laboring class
and kept company with sinners
and stood on the side of the dispossessed.
It is the poor, in His own words,
that shall inherit the kingdom of God.
One wonders where that leaves
the average churchgoing Christian today.

It is high time that God's children begin to recognize
who they are and really believe what they are
and begin demonstrating the joy of that relationship.
It is time that those who are baptized into Christ
stop rummaging for identity in the garbage heaps
of this world and begin to claim it.
They have identity.
"We are God's children now," wrote John.
According to Paul, *"has blessed* us in Christ . . .
chose us in Him before the foundation of the world . . .
destined us in love to be His sons through Jesus Christ . . .
appointed [us] to live for the praise of His glory . . .
sealed [us] with the promised Holy Spirit."
Christians have identify;
they need only begin to act like it.
The most attractive thing about a Christian is his joy—
and there is nothing in greater demand
in this sorrow-infested world
than the true note of joy which only Christians
can manifest honestly and confidently.

It is high time that Christians wake up and look up,
for salvation is nearer today than it has
ever been before.

They cannot afford to slumber within the smugness
of some former religious experience.
There must be incessant renewal and rededication
to the Person and the purposes of Jesus Christ.
Christians are living in the shadows
of the greatest event that shall ever
overtake this world.
Time is very short.
"Let us not sleep, as others do,
but let us keep awake and be sober. . . .
The Lord is at hand."